Man, This Is Living!

By Donna Bonkoski

Second Edition

By Donna Bonkoski

© 2018 by Donna Bonkoski

Edited by Connie Smith

ISBN: 978-1-387-76224-8

Table of Contents

Experience   *Page*

Experience 1. Donna Bonkoski

1a. Chapter 1

Have you ever come to the place where you didn't want to live anymore: Life was such a hassle and there seemed nothing in the future that even gave you a ray of hope for anything better? Then there was no one to talk to that understood your problems when you did share them?

Well, that was the situation I was in for three years. Life seemed utterly hopeless, and the future looked very black. I was married, 33 years old, and had six children from 6 years old to 15.

I did tell some friends, but they acted like they didn't believe me.

Here is how it all started:

It was a typical September evening at our house. After our evening meal was cleared away and our six children did their chores and homework, watched some television, they went off to bed. The television was turned off and the house became very quiet. After sitting at the kitchen table with my husband, reading the evening paper, I stood up and said, "I guess I'll go to bed: Morning comes pretty early." I folded up my part of the paper and walked toward the bedroom.

My husband said very firmly, "Just a minute. I want to talk to you."

I went back to the table and sat down. As I looked into his face and wondering what he wanted to talk to me about, I asked, "What is it?" (This was so unusual for him to say he wanted to talk to me, for he normally would just say whatever he wanted to tell me.)

He said, "Do you know so-and-so?" (He mentioned a man's name.)

I replied, "No, I don't. Who is he? Is he one of your new meat customers?"

His face got red with rage, and he snapped at me, "Don't act so innocent; you know who he is."

I said, "Look, I don't know anyone by that name. Who is he?"

"Don't tell me that; you do know. He's your boyfriend from Canada," he said.

As I looked at him, I couldn't believe the change that had come over him. He was almost out of control with anger. He didn't even look the same. He looked like a complete stranger, someone I didn't even know. We had been married 16 years, and I had never seen him act or look like this before.

"My what? I don't know anybody from Canada," I said shocked.

Then he began to name off men's names both in the neighborhood and others I'd never heard of.

As I sat there shaking, wondering what was going on, I couldn't get over the change in my husband's face. His eyes looked like those in a scary movie; they looked so strange. I kept thinking that this must be a bad dream and I would wake up and find out that I was having a nightmare.

But, it didn't stop. As I sat there, he kept on demanding that I confess to all these things he was accusing me of. I began to get very scared. I had never seen him act like this before, and it really frightened me.

"You had better confess; I'll understand," he yelled.

3

"Listen, I am not going to confess to anything; I didn't do anything. I don't know some of those people you have been talking about; and the men that I do know, I have not been having an affair with them. I haven't had an affair with anyone."

I tried to tell him, but he wouldn't listen. He just went right on raving about me and all my affairs with men. All these affairs were supposed to be of a sexual nature.

We lived in the country, and the few houses were far apart. So there were no close neighbors to hear any of this.

Have you ever seen something so horrifying that you couldn't believe that it was happening? Well, that is the way I felt. What is going on?

As he went on yelling at me and telling me to confess, I began to shake and cry. When that happened, he pointed his finger at me and snarled, "See, you must be guilty, or you wouldn't be crying!" And the more I professed my innocence, the more he was losing control.

I kept thinking to myself, "I really don't know this guy. What has happened to him?" This went on for four hours. I didn't think I had anymore tears left.

Finally, as abruptly as it started, it ended. And he said I could go to bed.

After I got into bed, I just lay there shaking. My heart was pounding so hard that I thought it would jump right out, and the pulse in my ears was so loud that I could hardly hear.

My husband didn't come to bed just then. He prowled around the house in the dark for a while.

I never knew that people could be so consumed with fear, but I was.

Finally, I went to sleep, and as I woke up the next morning, I looked over at my husband sleeping next to me so peacefully. And I thought, "Maybe it never happened: I must have had a nightmare. He looks alright today."

It wasn't a nightmare, because it didn't stop. It went on the next night-and-the-next and on-and-on every night for nearly six months. I could hardly eat, and I was shaking all the time.

People would come up to me at church and ask me if I was sick. I could not tell anyone what was going on at our house, as it was all too ridiculous. They wouldn't believe me.

After so many nights of interrogations and very little sleep, I felt like I could sleep for a week. It was several hours till the kids would get home from school, so I thought I'd just lay down for a little while. I locked the front door and the kitchen door and went into the bedroom and just lay across the bed for a short rest.

I must have gone to sleep immediately. I felt like someone was looking at me, and I woke up with a start.

My husband was standing by the bed, looking down at me. I was filled with fear, as no one else was around; and I thought, "I guess this is it: This is when he kills me."

"He said, "What are you doing laying on the bed?"

I lied and said I didn't feel good.

Then he said, "Well, the next time you lay down, you'd better be sure you lock all the doors. You didn't lock the utility room door." With that, he left the house.

I didn't sleep anymore that day, as I was so frightened and my heart was beating so fast. You'd have thought I'd been running for miles.

A few days later, I got to thinking that I didn't want to live if this was the way my life would be. I'd probably live till I was 90 and have to live with him that long. My mother always said, "Once you're married, you are married for life!"

Well, I didn't want to live with him for life, so I began thinking of ways to kill myself. I remembered how a neighbor had killed himself: He had taken a lot of pills, but they found him before he had died and pumped his stomach. So, then he had driven to an isolated spot and hooked a hose to his exhaust pipe and put it through the car window and died from the fumes.

I didn't get to use the car very often, so I knew I couldn't even consider that way. The only pills I had were aspirin, and I didn't know if they would work.

Then, I got to thinking that, if I did kill myself, "Who would take care of my six children?" My mother had died six months before, and my father was grieving. I had brothers and sisters, but they all had families and couldn't take on six kids.

I finally came to the conclusion that I'd have to stay alive and keep on living the way I was. I never told my children what was going on while they were sleeping.

One day, my older daughter asked me, "Mom, how come when Dad talks to someone on the phone, he talks so nice; but when he talks to us, he is not nice?"

I didn't know what to tell her, so I just said, "Oh, I guess he's just tired."

She never said any more about it.

1b. Chapter 2

After several months, I began to wonder if I might be crazy. My husband was telling me that I was all the time. He would tell me that I went here or there; and I knew I hadn't. I thought maybe I *was* crazy: They say that the last one to know that you're crazy is you. I thought I'd better find out, as I might hurt one of my children. So I made an appointment with our family doctor. I went in and had a complete physical check-up. After all the tests were finished, the doctor came into the room where I was.

He said, "Physically you are fine. You are a little underweight and you are very nervous, but other than that, you're fine." He pulled up a chair across from me and sat down. He took both of my hands in his and looked into my face.

Right then, I began crying.

He said, "Now, Donna, tell me what is going on at home."

I told him all the things that had been going on and asked him the question I was afraid to ask, "Doctor, am I crazy? If I am, please tell me, even if it hurts me."

He looked at me with so much compassion and said, "There is nothing wrong with you mentally. You are not crazy, but you will be if this kind of things keep up. You'd better get your husband to a psychiatrist; he needs help."

"He won't go; he says I'm the crazy one," I cried.

The doctor went on to tell me that he could give me something to calm me down, but I might not react quickly if something was to happen.

Relieved, I told him I wouldn't need anything as long as I knew that I wasn't crazy.

When my husband got home from work that day, he asked me what the doctor had said. Then, when I told him that I was all right and the doctor said that he should see a psychiatrist, he got angry and said, "There is nothing wrong with me. I've told you that you are the crazy one. I'm not going to any *head-doctor*. Do you understand?" And with that, he turned around and walked outside.

1c. Chapter 3

One night, as I sat in the kitchen and hearing my husband ranting on about me, he mentioned that, one day, a man had come into his meat-shop and told my husband that he'd just had a hot old time with me.

I thought, "There is a young man that works with my husband, and I'm going to try and go and talk to him and see if any such thing ever happened."

A few weeks later, I was going to choir practice. I had found out where this young man lived. I didn't go to choir practice; I went to find this young man.

They were having a birthday party at his house. There were some people standing outside, so I asked them if they would go and ask him if I could talk to him. They told him and he came out. I told him the story my husband told me, and he looked at me so shocked. He said, "Nothing like that ever happened."

I said, "Listen, if someone did say that, please tell me, because my husband insists it happened."

He replied, "I'm telling the truth. He must be working too hard. He needs a vacation."

I thanked him and asked him not to say anything about this to my husband. He said he would not say or do anything.

1d. Chapter 4

The nightly sessions continued every night for months until one night in February. I had gone to bed and was hoping that he wouldn't make me get up and have him yell at me.

He came to bed and lay there quietly. I thought that this night would be different, and maybe I would get some sleep.

I was nearly asleep when he said, "Do you remember the time you called me and asked me to bring home two loaves of bread?"

I thought, "Oh no, here we go again." I asked him what was so great about me asking him to bring home some bread. I did that often.

He said that I had told him I had had a sexual affair with a neighbor man back in the woods.

I got so angry and sat up and said, "You're crazy! You are just plain crazy!"

With that, he grabbed me around the throat and began choking me and yelling, "I'm not crazy. You're crazy."

It's amazing what went through my mind at that moment. I had felt that he would try to kill me sometime; but I thought he would either shoot me or stab me, because he had a revolver and lots of knives, as he was a butcher. I would have never thought about him chocking me. Then I thought that if he killed me, he would kill all the children. So I managed to wiggle around and fight my way from his grasp. I ran into the bathroom and locked the door. I had left some clothes in there just in case I would need them, and so I dressed in a hurry.

Meanwhile, he was right behind me, and as the door slammed in his face, he began to pound on it and was shouting, "You had better open this door. You are not going to get away from me this time. I am going to kill you."

Then I heard one of my children crying. My daughter, that was sleeping in the bedroom next to the bathroom, had awakened when she heard all the shouting. When I heard her crying, I thought, "What if he should turn on her and hurt her? I have to come out and face him." I opened the door, and he stood there just seething with anger. I pointed my finger at him and said with authority, "You get away from me, and don't you touch me!"

I think I must have shocked him, as I had never talked back to him and had always just let him tell me what to do.

He just stood there, looking surprised; and I turned and told my daughter that she was having a bad dream and to go back to sleep.

Then, my husband said, "Get out in the kitchen." And it started all over again with the accusations and his yelling at me. This went on till around two o'clock in the morning. I thought, if I lived until morning, I was going to do something so this would stop.

After my husband went to work and the children left for school, I thought that this awful nightmare had been going on for six months, and I couldn't stand it anymore.

I had told my story to several people, and I could see that they didn't believe me. My husband was acting so happy-and-nice out in public, and everyone seemed to think he was a great guy and I was imagining all this.

The next day, I was trying to figure out what had happened to him. I thought back to the time I met my husband. I had been working as a car-hop at a drive-in Root Beer stand; Barney delivered meat there.

He was engaged to a girl I worked with. The girl was so excited that she was going to be married soon to Barney. One day, her mother and Barney's mother met there with the girl to talk about the wedding. That is when her mother told Barney's mother that the girl was only 15 years old.

Well, the wedding was called off. The girl quit working there and left. Barney kept on delivering meat to the business.

One night, as we were closing, it began to rain real hard. I had six blocks to walk home, so my boss asked Barney to take me home. I told them I didn't need a ride, as I didn't mind a little rain.

They kept insisting, and so he drove me home. He asked me to go roller skating the next week, and I went with him; and that is how it all started.

Five months later, we were married. He was 21, and I was 17. It wasn't long before the babies began to arrive. Within 10 years, I had six children: 2 girls and 4 boys. I was super busy caring for this big family, and I don't know where my husband thought I had time for boyfriends or anything else.

Experience 2 The Pastor; The Doctor

2a. Chapter 5

I tried to think of someone who could help me, but at that time, there was no help for women in our area. I thought the last person that might help me was the pastor of the church I had attended for years.

My husband left the car home that day and drove his meat-truck to work. He worked as a butcher and meat-cutter at a wholesale meat-shop just down our road about ¼ of a mile. I would have to drive past the shop to get to the pastor's home, but fortunately, they were building a new road nearby. So I drove around that way so I wouldn't be seen.

In just a few minutes, I arrived at the pastor's home and hurried up and knocked on the door. (I thought if anyone could help me, it would be him.) He answered and invited me in.

I told him I had to talk to him.

He asked me to sit down and tell him what my problem was.

I began to shake and cry. I told him my husband had tried to kill me the night before; and if I had not managed to get away from him, he would have succeeded. I told him a little that had been going on in our home for the last five months.

He didn't say anything. He just stood there looking at me.

I said, "Pastor, you have got to help me!"

He just smiled and said, "You know, Donna, I like you and I like your husband; and I don't want to take sides."

I looked at him incredulously. I said, "I don't want you to take sides. Just tell me what I and the children should do." (Meanwhile, I was thinking in my mind, "He was my last hope, and now it looks hopeless.")

His wife was standing nearby listening, and she said, "You know what I think?"

I said, "No, Mary, what do you think?"

She replied, "I think he is trying to make you jealous. He is just kidding."

15

"Kidding? You think he was kidding when he was choking me? I don't think so. If I had not managed to get away from him, I wouldn't be here today asking for help."

They both just stood there looking at me and smiling. I could see they didn't believe me either. Then, the pastor said, "Have you heard of the Christian psychologist that comes once a week to a church in a nearby town? He comes from Detroit. Maybe he can help you."

I told him I would try anything.

He then went to the phone and proceeded to make an appointment for me. He handed me a slip of paper with the appointment time on it. It was for one month later on a Good Friday.

I thanked him and returned home.

2b. Chapter 6

When I left the pastor's home, I made a decision: I had to get out of the house.

My husband worked just ¼ mile down our road. He would come home for lunch; and quite often, he would check the gravel driveway for tire-tracks. (He was sure someone was coming to see me.)

Sometimes he would call on the phone; and if the line was busy, he would come home to see who I was talking to.

I very seldom used the phone, because we didn't have a private line. We were on an 8-person party-line, and it was always busy.

Anyway, I called my father as soon as I got home and asked him if I could come and work for him. He had a carpet-and-furniture cleaning business, and I had helped him before.

He asked me why I wanted to work out, and I began to cry. I told him what had been going on for the past five months, and he was shocked. He was quiet for a minute and then said, "You bring the kids and come and live with me." (My mom had died eight months before this, and he had lived alone.)

I told him, "No, that would just get you involved." (I knew my husband would make us all come back home.) I said, "If you would just let me come and work for you, it would give me a time to get out of the house so I could think a little and not be afraid of him being so close by."

He told me I could start the next day.

The next thing was to tell my husband.

When I told him, he just said, "Good, we can use the extra money."

It really helped me to get out of the house and not be so afraid all the time. I went to work regularly with my father, and just getting away really helped.

The day came for my appointment with the Christian psychologist. I left work early and told my father that, if my husband called, not to tell him where I had gone: Just tell him I had left.

This was a Good Friday, and my husband only had to work a half-day. The children would get out of school at noon, so they would all be home waiting for me.

I walked into the office of the psychologist, and the doctor had me fill out some papers with a lot of questions about how I felt about different things. Then he had me come into his office and had me tell him why I had come to see him.

I told him what had been going on for the past seven months and how I was so afraid of my husband and how he had tried to choke me. Then I waited for him to tell me what to do. I told him all I could in half an hour, and he said, "I have to talk to your husband too."

I told him my husband would never come, for he had told me that I was crazy.

The doctor said, "If I don't talk to him, I can't help you."

I told him to give me an appointment card for us both, but I didn't think he would come.

After receiving the appointment card, I was taken to another room with a desk and a chair in it. He handed me several papers and a pencil and asked me to sit down and do this psychological test. After he walked out, I looked over the pages and began to fill in the answers. By the time I got finished and went home, it was late in the afternoon.

When I got home that day, my husband was waiting. "Where were you? I called your father, and you were not there," he hollered.

I calmly told him that I had been to a Christian psychologist, and my husband said, "You need one."

I replied, "So do you. I have an appointment for you next Thursday when I go, and if you don't go, I'll divorce you."

He just stood there, stunned; and he didn't say anything for a minute. Then he just turned around and went outside.

I shocked myself saying that, as I had never ever thought about divorce.

Finally, he came back inside as I was making our supper, and he asked what time the appointment was. He said he would drive the truck, and I could drive the car.

I was really surprised he had said he would go.

2c. Chapter 7

We both drove separately to the doctor's appointment. It was always on Friday at 2:00 p.m. The doctor had my husband come in the first half hour, and then he would leave. And I would be called in the last half hour. The doctor would then say, "Why did you say those things to him and why did you do those things?"

I tried to tell the doctor that I hadn't done anything or said anything to him. I tried to explain that I don't even talk to him. If I want to ask him something, I send one of the kids to ask him, and I certainly did not do the things he said I did.

The doctor said I needed to be extra nice to him.

My husband would tell the doctor such lies. Then, every week, when I would go in to the doctor, I would end up defending myself.

One Thursday, the doctor said to me, "You are a Christian, and you have to love your husband. You go home and read 1 Corinthians Chapter 13 every day, and then come back and tell me you love your husband."

So I did that and finally said, "Lord, why did you put that in the Bible? I hate him."

Every time I went to see the doctor, he would ask, "Well, do you love him?"

I would answer with, "I hate him."

The doctor would say, "You have to love your husband."

I said, "Listen here. Do you think I like living like this? If I could find the "love-button," I would push it. I will live with him until the kids are grown. Then I will go my way and he can go his."

2d. Chapter 8

After we had been seeing this doctor, and I was always the bad guy, I just told him that we would not be coming anymore. It had been nearly two years, and my husband was bringing him steaks; and he was always the good guy and I was always the terrible wife.

At that time, the state decided to build an interstate highway through where we lived, and they wanted our property for an exit. So we had to move.

We did not go to the doctor anymore, but my husband continued to take him steaks every Thursday. On my last appointment with the doctor, I just casually asked him, "What do I do if he tries to kill me again?"

He said, "Oh, I don't think he will."

I replied, "Well, just suppose."

His exact words to me were, "Just have him thrown in the can."

I said, "Oh? What do I do when he gets out?" Then I said, "See! It didn't do me any good to come to you. You just wasted my time and money."

One time later, after I was born again, the pastor of that church said to me as I was delivering the doctor's steaks, "You don't come anymore. How did you get your problem solved?"

I just told him I was born again and the Lord took care of it.

He just hmphed and walked away.

The doctor finally told me, after much questioning on my part, that my husband was hearing voices and was a Paranoid Schizophrenic.

Experience 3. Building A New House
(Chapter 9)

As I said earlier, the state needed our property to make an exit for a new highway, and so the move for us was on. I began just driving around looking for property to build our new house on, and I wasn't finding anything.

One night at church, I said something about my hunting for property. One of the ladies said, "You can buy some property from us." She said her husband had said they didn't need all the land they had, and he would like to sell some.

The next day, I went over to their home and bought three acres from them. The property contained mostly woods, and so we cleared an area and hired a contractor to frame the house in. We didn't have any plans for a house. So my husband had said, "You just draw out what you want."

I knew we needed 4 bedrooms and 2 bathrooms and the other rooms, and so I drew it out on paper. The builders went by the paper as I had drawn it. I went to a large lumber yard in a small town called Romeo and picked out the windows-and-doors and was told they would be delivered to our property. I also picked out the siding and the roofing.

The state was in a hurry about our leaving our present home, and so a person from the state said we could rent it from the state for $35.00 per month. When he came to pick up his money, he had penciled in $85.00 instead. At that time, we could have rented a 4-bedroom house for $90.00. The man would not back down, and so I gave him the $85.00. We stayed for one month and had to leave.

We moved into the new home as they were sanding down the drywall. The entire family got busy with painting and insulation and the installing of the flooring and everything else we had to do to make it livable.

In the meantime, my husband quit accusing me, as I told him if he did, I would call the doctor; and that seemed to work.

The kids and I still went to the same church, and our lives were very busy: The kids had school and my husband went to work and I worked on the house.

One day, just before supper-time, my husband came in from work. I was sawing a piece of trim to put around a window, and I was having a hard time. Melanie, my daughter, said to her dad, "Dad, why don't you help Mom?

He replied, "She is doing all right." He then went in to watch television.

He told me later, "If you want this house finished, you finish it. I am through with it!"

After this, I learned to do the electrical plugs, the lights, the shower, the bi-fold closet doors, and everything else.

Experience 4. Janitor

4a. Chapter 10

As I was the cleaning-person for the church, I had the opportunity to talk to the pastor often. One day, I asked him, "Pastor, I thought when you got "saved," something happened: You felt different or things changed." (I had been reading Christian books in the church library, and the stories always told how things were different.)

He just laughed and said, "You just take it by faith. You tell yourself you are saved, and you're saved."

One day, I started talking to him and told him it didn't do me any good to come to church. Why be a Christian if nothing is different? I said, "I am just going to quit coming. It doesn't do me any good."

He laughed and said, "That is what the devil wants you to do."

I said, "Maybe I am not doing enough."

At that time, I was a Sunday school teacher, the janitor, I played the piano and the organ, was in the choir, helped with the Junior Choir, and sang in the Ladies Trio.

He said, "We are going to start a youth-group. You might want to do that."

I told him, "If something doesn't happen, I am quitting and staying home."

He just laughed and went into his office.

In a previous conversation with him, I had asked, "Why don't you ever preach on the *Book of Acts*?" And he had said, "That is just history."

A short time after I had spoken to the pastor, I picked up the local newspaper and saw an ad about some ex-drug addicts. They were going to be at a church nearby on Wednesday night. I thought that it was impossible to get off drugs, but this ad said they had done just that.

Because it was Wednesday, I called my youngest daughter Melanie into the room and said, "We are going to a different church tonight."

She said that was okay with her. She was 11 years old, and she would go to church with me on Wednesday nights. While I was at choir practice, she would play with the other kids.

That night, we attended a different church. When we arrived, there were only a few seats left. The ushers took us down about half way, and when we sat down, I was surprised to see one of the ladies from my other church sitting there. We laughed because we both had skipped our regular Wednesday night service.

The music leader had everyone sing a few songs. Then he turned the service over to the leader of "Teen Challenge." Their leader said, "Now, these boys are going to act out a five-act play," and the play began.

It was very life-like. They had big hypo needles, and they would tie a rag around their arms before they gave themselves a shot. This was their own life-story: They would fight with each other and steal. And they told the things they had done in the past. They acted out what it was like to be a slave to drugs. It was a terrible thing to watch, and I wondered how anyone could be saved from a life like that.

Toward the last part of the play, one of the young men was persuaded to go to a Teen Challenge place and was converted or saved. The others also had the same experience by what they called the "Power of the Holy Ghost." They had become free from all the desire for drugs.

I thought, "Wow, this is fantastic."

When the play ended, the pastor (leader) asked the young men to go and change their clothes and come back. And each one gave his personal testimony of what God had done for him.

One of them had been on heroin for around 16 years and had taken the cure in Lexington and had been in San Quentin Prison and other jails, but as soon as he got out, he would go right back on drugs again. He had been married and had two little girls. His wife got so upset with him that she divorced him and moved to South America. She didn't even want to be in the same country with him.

I was shocked at the things I was hearing. I never really knew anything about such a life. When each man had told his story, the last fellow (tall, loose-jointed, gangly) stepped forward, and all he said was, "Man, this is living!"

That struck a chord in me, and I thought, "That is what I want!" I want some living. I am tired of this slow death.

When I left that church on that night, I was determined to find some *living*.

4b. Chapter 11

The next morning, I called the head of the trustees of my church. I told him to find a new janitor, as I was quitting. He wanted to know why, and I said, "I'm going to find some living."

He said, "We've got living in our church."

I replied, "Frank, I've been in this church for 17 years, and I haven't found any living yet. So I am going to look someplace else."

I continued, "I will clean the church this weekend, but that is the last time. I will also sing in the Ladies Trio on Sunday morning: That is it; I am done."

The following Sunday morning, I was at church, knowing that it was my last time. Of course, the word had gotten around that I was leaving.

After the morning service, another Sunday school teacher came to me and said she would leave too, but her parents had always gone to this church, and she couldn't leave. She asked me where I was going.

I told her I was going to find some living.

Then she said, "Where are you going tonight?"

I told her I had heard about a little church in the north end of town nearby. I had heard it was really different there. I thought I'd go from one extreme to the other extreme. I said, "If I don't find it, I'll just stay home." I couldn't see any future in sitting in a church the rest of my life and being miserable.

The church people watched me leave. They were talking among themselves about how mixed up Donna was, and they would have to pray for me. They didn't know that Mary, the wife of the head of the trustees (and who I sang in the trio with) was the one who told me about the little church.

Mary called me Sunday afternoon and said, "If you will drive over to my house, I will drive you to that other little church. Frank is going to take the kids and go to the Baptist church, and I will go with you to the Pentecostal church."

I had never heard of a Pentecostal church, but I said, "Okay, I will drive over and ride with you."

As we drove along the expressway, she said, "They don't wear any make-up there."

I said, "Oh, I only have lipstick on." Then I grabbed a hanky and wiped it across my lips. "All right; I'm ready," I said.

4c. Chapter 12

As we drove along, Mary told me more about what she had seen when she went to that church, "They clap their hands and raise them high and say, '*Praise the lord*'; and they wash each other's feet when they had a 'foot-washing'." Then she went on to say, at times, they would have a "Jericho March" around in the church.

What she said didn't make any impression on me, as I had no idea what she was talking about.

She also told how the pastor there would go help the people shovel snow from their yards. And in the summer, he would go mow their lawns.

I couldn't imagine our pastor doing anything like that. He just waited for someone else to come and do those things for him.

As Mary drove into the parking lot at the church, I could hear music. It sounded real nice and much peppier than the music at our church. Mary and I got out of the car and walked over to the double doors.

The music was wonderful. There was a lady playing the piano, and another lady was playing the organ. They were up on the platform. There were people kneeling all around the platform (they called it the "altar"). They were all praying out loud and crying. I had never seen a church like this. Mary and I found a seat near the back and sat down to wait for the service to begin.

4d. Chapter 13

I just sat there trying to take this all in when Mary said, "We'd better go down and pray too."

So we walked down front and knelt down in an open spot. It didn't take us long to do our praying. Then we walked back to where we had been sitting and sat down.

The people began to go to their seats, and a lady went over and stood behind the pulpit. She opened a song book and asked everyone to turn to the page with the song they were going to sing. The song leader turned out to be Mary's neighbor. She was the person that had introduced Mary to the church.

The singing was wonderful. I just sat there and watched. Some raised their hands in praise, and I thought, "I'm not going to raise my hands." (I bit my fingernails all my life, and I didn't want anyone to see them.)

Then they began to sing *How Great Thou Art*. To me, it seemed there was an unseen power slowly whirling around in there, and the power kept getting stronger until I looked up at the ceiling. I thought this power was going to lift the roof off. I just kept looking up at the ceiling, but nothing happened.

After a wonderful time of music, things settled down, and I felt that power settled down too. After some announcements, the pastor began to speak. He was a young man, and he seemed to just be full of energy. He didn't stay up on the platform or behind the pulpit. He was down in front by the people.

He had only been speaking a short time when there was a commotion behind us at the entrance of the church. The pastor stopped speaking, and everyone looked around to see what was happening.

A woman, very drunk, was trying to make her way up the steps, and she was holding onto the railing to help her. She managed to stagger to a seat which was right across from me. And I thought, "I wonder what they are going to do about this."

It was very quiet for a moment, and then the pastor said, "Oh, Blanche, have you let the devil get you all messed up again? You better get down here to the altar and ask God to forgive you."

She just sat there.

Then the pastor said, "A couple of you men help her down to the altar."

4e. Chapter 14

Then the pastor began to tell us that this lady had had a wonderful saving experience a while back at a tent-meeting, but every time she went back to see her family, she would get drunk. Every time this happened, she would always go someplace to have God forgive her. The pastor stopped for a minute and then said, "You know, there are a lot of you others that need to get some things straightened out with God too."

The people began to get up and head for the altar. The pastor asked Mary and another lady to go and pray with Blanche, so I sat there alone, except for a few little kids. I thought, "Well, I haven't found any living here, so where will I go next time?"

About that time, the pastor was standing in front of me. He said, "Say, Sister, wouldn't you like to pray too?"

I thought, "He's going to think I am a heathen if I don't." I stood up and followed him down the altar. There was just a small spot where no one was kneeling, so I knelt down there. Another lady came and knelt beside me. My knees just hit the floor when I began to burst out sobbing.

The pastor was standing in front of me and said, "Sister, just tell God what you want. He's got it."

I looked up and said, "Oh God, I don't know what I want. I'm a mess. Just fix me up." It seemed like there was a storm going on inside of me, and I kept thinking, "There is no way out of this mess, God! Please help me!"

I was at the altar for hours. After a long time, crying and begging God to help me, it seemed like everything inside of me calmed down. The storm was gone. I thought, "I don't have to cry anymore. Everything is going to be all right."

I looked up, and the pastor was standing before me. He said, "Thank God, Sister, you've got it."

I stood up, and Mary was there. She said, "Did you get it?"

I said, "I think so. The pastor said I got it."

Mary said, "Did you speak in another language?"

I said, "I don't think so."

Then she said, "You didn't get it."

I said, "I got something. I sure feel good."

4f. Chapter 15

About that time, I felt a bubble coming up into my throat, and it was laughter. I had not laughed in such a long time, and it felt so good.

There were only a few people left at the church. I had been kneeling there for over three hours.

Mary said, "We've got to go home. It is after 11:00 p.m."

We went out to the car and headed for home, and I just kept laughing.

Finally, Mary said, "You had better stop that laughing, or Barney really will kill you tonight."

I said, "I don't care. He can cut me up in little pieces and put me through the meat grinder and feed me to the dogs." (I kept on laughing.)

When we got to Mary's house, I got into my car and drove the few miles home. I laughed all the way, knowing things were going to be different from now on. I didn't know what had happened to me, but I felt wonderful!

Experience 5. The Holy Laughter

(Chapter 16)

As I opened the front door and walked in, I realized that I felt very strange. I had been laughing for nearly an hour, and I felt silly. I was weak, and I leaned against the wall and sort of slid myself along toward the kitchen.

I hadn't heard anything about being drunk in the Spirit. If I had, I would have known what was happening to me.

I usually got out of church early, and so my husband was waiting for me. It was nearly midnight. He got up from the kitchen table where he had been sitting and came over near me. He studied me for a second and then he snarled at me, "Are you drunk?"

I was giggling, "Of course not, you know that I never have drank! I can't even stand the smell of that stuff -- ha-ha-ha."

"Well, you sure act like it," he answered and looked disgustedly at me. "Where have you been?"

Still laughing, I said, "I have been to church."

After a few seconds, he whirled around and said, "I am going to bed; you are nuts!" Then he started for the bedroom.

I said to him, "Wait a minute! I want to tell you something."

He turned to face me and said, "Well, what do you want?"

I replied, "I just want to tell you that I love you!" Then I began to break into laughter. I threw my arms out and said, "I love everybody!"

A look of bewilderment came over his face, and he said with contempt, "Now I know you are nuts! I am going to bed." (This was Halloween night of 1965.)

I went into the kitchen, still laughing. I couldn't stop laughing. I knew this was really irritating my husband, so I tried to stop. I got the dish towel and put it over my mouth, and the laughter burst out. I kept telling myself that I must stop laughing, but I couldn't.

In a short time, my husband was so angry that he called me from the bedroom and told me that I'd better shut up and come to bed.

I tried to tell him that I couldn't stop laughing, and he just kept on yelling at me to shut up and come to bed.

I got ready for bed and went into the bedroom and got into bed. I knew that my husband was just steaming: He was so angry at me. I put the pillow over my head and still laughed. I pushed some of the cover into my mouth, and the laughter still burst out. I thought that my husband would probably like to ring my neck, but I didn't even care. He could hurt me if he wanted to, and I didn't care. I thought I would never go to sleep, as I felt so wonderful; but eventually I did.

Experience 6. The First Day of Living
(Chapter 17)

The next morning, I woke up still laughing. I got dressed and hurried out into the kitchen. As I looked out the kitchen window over the sink, I noticed that everything outside looked different. The trees looked like they glistened, and the grass looked like sprigs of velvet.

I ran and woke the children and told them to hurry out into the kitchen and look out the window. They stood all around me and asked me what I wanted them to see.

I said, "Don't the trees look beautiful?"

They said that they didn't look any different to them. It looked like the same old grass.

My oldest daughter was 17, and she looked at me. She acted like she was studying me and trying to figure me out. Then she said, "You know what I think, Mom?"

I looked at her, and I could tell what she was thinking. I laughed and said, "What do you think?"

She said cautiously, "I think you are cracking up."

I said, "Hey, if this is crazy, I wish I'd been crazy a long time ago. This is wonderful!"

My husband got up and they all had breakfast. And as my husband was eating his breakfast, he kept watching me. I guess he was trying to figure out what had happened to me.

They all left for work and school, probably wondering what kind of a mother they would find when they got home that day.

Everyone in my family just kind of stood back away from me for the next few days. They didn't know what to think of this new mother. Very strange, for she used to cry and shake. And now she laughs and is so happy and talks different. Very different!

Experience 7. The Bible is Real!

(Chapter 18)

That day after all the family had left for school and work, I got my Bible and thought I would take a look at it and see if things seemed any different. It seemed, before this strange and wonderful experience, when I would try to read the Bible, it didn't make much sense to me. This day, as I opened it up and turned the pages, everything was different. I turned to John 3:16 and read it. All of a sudden, I understood. It really surprised me. I realized that Jesus had died for ME! It really touched me to think that He would die for me. I began to cry as I thought of Him suffering such a horrible death and I didn't deserve it.

Finally, I just let the Bible flop open wherever it wanted to, and the page turned to 2 Corinthians 5:17. It seemed to be in bold, black, raised-up print, "If any man be in Christ, he is a new creature: Old things are passed away; behold, all things become new."

All things are become new? That's what happened to me! Everything looks different! I feel different too!

I smacked my hand against my forehead and said, "You-stupid-idiot, you have just been born again. How could you have been so dumb to think you were saved before and your life had never changed?" All this time I thought I had been saved, and I hadn't been saved at all. Oh, the mercy of God.

I used to ask people about salvation. I would say, "I thought that something happened when you got saved, . . . that you felt different or something." I always got the answer, "Well, you take it by faith. You just keep telling yourself that you are saved, and you are saved."

Well, my life had really changed last night! Now I realized what that young man had meant the night he said, "Man, this is living!" I had just found my living! My life had changed. I felt different. Everything looked different. No, I looked the same, but I would never be the same again! I was starting a new life all over again.

When this happened, no one had to tell me what had happened. The Bible had told me. Such pure joy! Such happiness! *Praise the Lord*!

Right then, I told the Lord that I would do anything, go any place, say anything He wanted me to say, no matter what. I was so grateful for what He had done for me!

Experience 8. New Friends in Christ!
(Chapter 19)

Then I thought of all the years I had wasted. Thirty-six years old, and I finally woke up. I went to the phone and called Mary, "Mary, do you know what happened to me last night?"

She said, "Well, I know you sure were happy."

I said, "Mary, I was born again last night. I feel different, and everything looks different. I even love my husband, and the Bible makes sense to me now. This one verse stuck up in bold print, and it said, 'If a man is in Christ, he is a new creature. Old things are passed away and all things become new.' Mary, that is what happened to me. I've found my living."

She agreed that something had happened to me. She then suggested that we go over to her neighbor's and talk to her.

We met over at Betty's house, and when I told her what had happened to me, she laughed and said, "That is just like what happened to me when I was saved."

When she said that, I realized that being born again and being saved was the same thing.

Mary and I went over to Betty's house for the next few days. We learned so much from her. She shared her experiences and her knowledge of the Bible. We would sit and talk for hours, and we were making our souls and spirits fat.

She would fix a lunch and I would never eat, as I was never hungry. Later, I understood that I was fasting. My husband would say, "You'd better eat, or you are going to be sick."

I would just tell him, "Why eat if you're not hungry."

Experience 9. Another Miracle
(Chapter 20)

I had suffered with a gall bladder condition for many hears and couldn't eat tuna fish without getting violently ill. I had said to my husband some weeks before this, "I don't care if we don't have any hospitalization. I've got to have an operation to have my gall bladder removed. I'm taking three times as many pills as I should, and I'm still sick all the time. I am so sick of being sick."

The following Sunday night, when I came home from church, I opened the front door and walked inside. I could smell tuna fish. It smelled so good, and I realized I was hungry. . . real hungry. I hadn't eaten for one week, because the Lord had me on a fast. My daughter

Terry was in the kitchen making a tuna fish sandwich. I walked over by her and said, "That sure smells good."

She said, "Mom, you know if you eat this, you'll be sick."

I said, "Yes, I know." I picked up the dish to put it in the fridge, and as I put my hand on the fridge handle, I remembered what the preacher said that night, "If you can believe for something, you can have it."

I said, "I believe I am healed, and so I'm healed."

I took the dish and set it on the counter and took two slices of bread and made me a big sandwich with that tuna fish.

Terry watched me and said, "Mom! Don't eat that. You'll be sick."

I said, "If I believe I'm healed, I'm healed." I thought, "If this is faith, . . . well, I don't feel anything." (I later found out that you don't feel faith: You just do the thing you are believing for, and God does the rest.)

I took my sandwich over to the table and began eating. Before I was through, I had eaten two tuna fish sandwiches. The rest of the family came out to watch me. My husband said, "There's not gonna be any sleeping tonight: She's gonna be in the bathroom throwing up all night."

I was healed that night. He said that I was going to die that night for sure, and I laughed and left them standing there with their mouths open. Poor Mother, she sure is crazy now.

The next morning, the kids ran into the bedroom and said, "Were you sick last night, Mom?"

I answered them laughing, "Now, if you believe you are healed, then you're healed, and you can see I am healed."

They didn't take my word for it, and so they asked their father. He answered, "She didn't move all night long. She wasn't sick at all."

I never had any problems with anything I've eaten since then. Thank you, Lord!

Experience 10. What a Wonderful Life!
(Chapter 21)

Every day was so exciting. I would get down and pray after my family left in the morning and ask God what He wanted me to do that day. As I prayed, I would find the leading of the Holy Spirit. Sometimes it would be to call someone on the phone, and other times He would have me go and visit someone. I always did what He said, and it would work out perfectly every time. It seemed that the person was waiting for me to call on them.

Each day was just so glorious. All I wanted to do was read my Bible. I was so hungry for the word of God. I would read it like a hungry man eats food. I'd read everything: The Concordance, the dictionary, and any comments on the last pages. I started getting up at 5:30 a.m. so I would be through praying before my family got up.

One morning, after everyone left for work and school, I asked the Lord what He wanted me to do that day. He said, "Call your former pastor." (Where I had attended church for 17 years.)

I said, "What will I say to him, Lord? He has been to Bible school, and he can talk circles around me."

Then He reminded me of what I had said to Him: I would do anything he told me to do, say anything He told me to say, and go anyplace He told me to go.

I thought a minute and said, "That's right, Lord. So I'll dial the phone, but you're going to have to tell me what to say, because I don't know why I'm calling him."

I heard the phone buzzing on the other end, and he answered the phone.

I said, "Hi, Pastor, this is Donna."

He seemed very surprised. He said, "Well, we wondered what happened to you." (This was on a Monday morning, and I'd only been gone for a week.)

I said, "All right, you'd better sit down, as this will take about an hour-and-a-half."

I went on to tell him how I had come to him for help and he couldn't help me. Then we went to this doctor he had suggested and that had done no good. So I went to a different church, and I had cried out to God at the altar and God saved me and gave me a born-again experience.

He said, "No, you were saved before."

I said, "I was never saved like this. I told you that I hated my husband before, and now I love him. I told you that I never had any prayers answered; and now, when I pray, I get an answer right away. I have a new life, and it's wonderful."

He said, "Well, we want you to come back; we need you."

I replied, "You don't want me to come back, Pastor: I'm not the same old Donna you knew before. I've told the Lord I would do anything He tells me to do and I'll go anywhere He sends me, and say anything He tells me to say."

Later that day, Mary called. Someone had just called her and said that the pastor had called a friend and told that person that they should pray for Mrs. Bonkoski, as she has gone off the deep end.

I also found out that the church board-members had said that, if I didn't come back to the church on Sunday night, they would call on me as a church-board on Monday night, and they would straighten me out.

That is why the Lord had me call the pastor on Monday morning. The Lord was guiding me already.

Experience 11. Get the House in Order
(Chapter 22)

As I got so wrapped up in my spiritual walk, some of my home chores got neglected. I didn't do any of the things like dish-washing or making the beds, and the house was beginning to show signs of neglect.

One day, my husband commented on my disorder, "If you don't get busy, I'm going to take the car away."

"Oh, that's all right," I replied.

"Then I'll have the phone taken out," he said.

I just smiled at him and said, "All right; I don't mind."

"Then what will you do then?' he said.

As I laughed, I said, "Oh, I'll just go out on the road and stand there and shout as loud as I can, 'Hey everybody, Jesus loves you!'"

He thought he was going to get me angry, and it didn't work. After that, I did manage to get all my chores done before I did my phoning or traveling around.

Every day was a new adventure. There were never two days the same. When I went to bed, I wanted to sleep fast so I could get started on the next day. I didn't want to waste any more time. There was so much to be done, and I wanted to tell others how wonderful it was to be born again. It was like blinders or scales were off my eyes. All of a sudden, I could see things so much better and so clearly now. What a difference Jesus makes. Oh, what a privilege it is to be a Child of the King! I could hardly wait for the next church service. I was learning so much and experiencing so much also.

Experience 12. A Wonderful Healing
(Chapter 23)

One evening, just a few weeks after my born-again experience and my healing of my gall bladder trouble, I was busying myself in the kitchen. It was after 9:00 p.m., and the three younger children had gone to bed. The others were busy with their school homework. Michael, the oldest one, was getting ready to go to work. He worked nights in a factory, and my husband wasn't home.

As I was doing some last-minute touching up in the kitchen, Melanie (who was 11 years old) came out of her bedroom. She had her pajamas on and had been in bed already. She came to me and said, "Mom, I've been thinking: If God can heal you, why can't He heal me?"

I thought a minute and said, "Well, I'm sure He can!"

With that, she turned around and went back into her bedroom. I saw her kneel down by the side of her bed and pray.

Two years previous to this, Melanie had started to have violent headaches. She would lie on the couch and complain every time someone would walk by or made a noise. I made an appointment with a doctor and took her there for a check-up. After a thorough examination, the doctor said Melanie was having migraine headaches. (I thought only older people had this problem.)

Then, I asked him what could be done for her to make her feel better.

He told me that there was nothing that would heal the problem. I could give her aspirin for the pain, and that would help as much as anything.

I couldn't believe what I was hearing. I said, "Do you mean to tell me that a nine-year-old child has to just suffer with this?"

He told me he was very sorry, but there wasn't anything else he could do for her.

I couldn't believe Melanie would have to go on suffering every few weeks when she got one of these headaches. The headache didn't just come for a day: She would be sick for days. This would be accompanied with vomiting also. She would miss three or four days of school at a time. That year, she missed so many days that she didn't nearly pass into the next higher grade.

I talked to a man whose mother had had migraine headaches, and he said she got relief by going to a chiropractor. I called and made an appointment with a local chiropractor.

Melanie had several treatments when she first started to go there, and then longer periods between treatments, as it seemed to be taking care of the headaches.

While we were building our new house and getting moved into it and settled, we sort of forgot about Melanie's appointment. She had a violent migraine headache that put her to bed for days. After that, I watched her appointments very closely.

Then, two years later, on the night that Melanie asked me if God could heal her, she was very sincere. The following night, I looked into Melanie's room, and she was kneeling again at her bedside praying. She prayed earnestly every night. And then, one day, she said, "Mom, have you noticed I haven't had any more headaches, and I haven't gone for any more treatments either?"

I said, "Why, that's right. You haven't."

"I believe that God has healed me, Mom," she said with a big smile on her face.

God did truly heal her. She never had another migraine headache after that: *Never!*

The following summer, Melanie went to church-camp with some of the kids from our church. One of the fathers had gone and picked up several of the campers and brought them home. When his car drove into the yard and stopped, Melanie couldn't get out of the car fast enough. She began yelling, "Mom! I got filled with the Holy Ghost, Mom. I got filled with the Holy Ghost."

She was sure filled with power all right. She was like a live wire, bouncing from here to there. God had surely blessed my little 11-year-old daughter.

The Bible says in Acts 2:39, "This promise of the Holy Ghost is to you and your children and to anyone who God would call."

Experience 13. God's Amazing Supply
(Chapter 24)

One winter day, as my children finished their breakfast, they hurried around gathering their books, lunches, and jackets getting ready to catch the school bus. Getting my change-purse out, I handed each one their milk-money for their lunch. In a flurry, they were out the door and running down the road to the school-bus stop. After standing at the window and seeing the bus go by with my children waving in the window, I turned back to my daily routine.

I cleared the dishes and breakfast clutter off the table and noticed the cereal box was empty. I walked over to the cupboard and checked it out and said, "Lord, You can see that was the last of the cereal and the bread for the school lunches. And You know, Lord, that I also need sugar, flour, peanut butter, milk, cereal, and so many other things."

I just kept telling Jesus what our needs were. I found that, after paying the bills that week, there were just a few pennies left, and that was what I had given the children for their milk money.

I picked up my Bible and took it into the living room and got down on my knees and began to talk to the Lord, "You know, Lord, it says in the Bible that You are concerned about the flowers and the sparrows."

While I was saying these things, I opened my Bible to that scripture in Matthew 6:26. I pointed to those verses and said, "Lord, if You want us to have groceries this week, You'll have to provide them for us, as I have just given the last of the money to the children."

While I was talking, the phone rang. It was my friend who rode to church with me. The name we all called her was Sister Fountain, a wonderful black lady. She told me she had a phone call from a friend who needed someone to take her to her daughter's home. Her daughter was pregnant, and she had gone into labor and had no one to watch her children so she could go to the hospital. The mother didn't have a car, as her husband dove it to work. She asked me to drive her there.

I said I could take her. I didn't have any money, but I had some gas in the car.

I ran out and got into the car and quickly drove over to our friend's home. She was waiting outside and got into the car. She was concerned that she wouldn't get there soon enough. When we got at her daughter's home, the cab was waiting. The mother got out and turned and threw something in onto the car seat.

I backed the car out of the driveway and started to drive away. I looked to see what she had thrown in onto the seat: It was a bill all folded up. I stopped the car to see what it was. I unfolded the bill and smoothed it out and found it was a five-dollar bill. I began to cry and said, "Lord, I didn't know You were going to answer so soon."

I sat there for a few minutes and thought that, as long as I was downtown, I would stop by the insurance company. My oldest son was now in the army and needed some information about his car insurance, so I decided to stop by there.

When I walked into the office, the lady at the desk said, "Mrs. Bonkoski, I was going to mail you this check. I found that there was a mistake last June, and we owe you $15.00." She picked up the check and handed it to me. Here it was January, and this is a mistake from last June.

I began to thank and praise the Lord, and she just sat there smiling. I told her I just had a talk with the Lord less than an hour ago about needing some groceries, and He has already given me $20.00. This is the amount I spent a week for groceries. (This was 1966; we got our meat where my husband worked.)

After getting the information about Mike's car insurance, I left and drove to the grocery store where I always shopped. Getting a grocery cart, I began putting the different things in the cart that I needed. Always before, I would keep a running-total so I'd be sure to get just what I could pay for. But this time, the Lord knew just what I needed, so I was sure He gave me enough money. After getting the things we needed, I said, "Lord, I'm just going to get a little candy for the kids."

Pushing my cart up to the counter, where a friend was a clerk, she said, "Hey! You never come shopping on Monday."

I replied, "Well, I wasn't going to get any groceries this week. But I had a talk with the Lord, and He provided the money for all of this."

She asked me if I wanted her to give me the subtotal like I always did, and I told her "No," as I knew the Lord had given me enough to pay for it. She rang up the total, and it came to $19.94. I just said, "*Praise the Lord*!"

After I arrived home and put all the groceries away, I could hardly wait for the kids to get home from school. Their first stop, when they got in the door, was the refrigerator.

I kept busy all day and just kept praising the Lord for His goodness. Later, I heard the front door open, and in-bounded my four youngest children. As they always did, they headed for the refrigerator. Pulling the door open, they let out a gasp, "Mom, where did you get all these groceries? I thought you said you didn't have any more money."

I told them that I was praying, and Sister Fountain called to ask if I would take Sister Anderson to her daughter's so she could watch the children, and she gave me some money. Then, as I went to check on Mike's car insurance, the lady gave me a check, and I went and bought the groceries and had just enough money to pay for them.

Kevin shouted, "Isn't God great? He answers prayer and gives us what we need."

We all agreed with him. And they talked about that to anyone who would listen for weeks.

Experience 14. Donna Does a No-No!
(Chapter 25)

This wonderful experience of being born again began on a Sunday night, which was also Halloween, 1965. On the following Friday night, the little church (where I had met the Lord) was having a birthday party at the church for their pastor. Also, in that meeting, a missionary (who was also a Bible school teacher and was being used greatly for the Lord) was beginning two weeks of meetings.

I had persuaded my husband to go with me to this party.

I had spent some time that day getting my long hair cut and fixed into a short style so I would have more time for the Lord. I wasn't aware of the "No-No" of not cutting one's hair.

When I arrived, different people said, "Oh, you got your hair cut."

I said, "Yes, I don't want to spend a lot of time fixing my hair, as I need all my time for the Lord."

The following Sunday at church, one of the old saints got up and told about how terrible it is for women to "bob" their hair.

Well, I felt like crawling under the seat, but I decided that my hair would grow fast, and besides, there was nothing I could do about it anyhow.

That evening, we began the special meetings, and they were glorious. The most interesting thing about it all was that I would study the Bible during the day, and the missionary would preach on the same scriptures that evening. I would ride to church with some of the ladies, and I would announce to them what the sermon would be about ahead of time. Sure enough, it would always be the same. I couldn't explain it then, and I can't explain it now. But then, I couldn't explain a lot of things.

Experience 15. The Joy of The Lord
(Chapter 26)

Life was so exciting: Every day was so new and different. The joy of the Lord is our strength, and I had so much joy. I said to my husband one day, "I feel like I could move mountains today."

He looked at me and said, "Well, then get out in the backyard and move some of those loads of sand around and level them off."

Well, that wasn't what I had in mind, but I praised the Lord as I leveled those loads of sand out in the back and front yards. There were ten large loads of sand delivered, and I and the children worked to level them all.

I enjoyed the most menial jobs after I had been born again. Nothing was too hard for me, as the Lord was right there with me. I'd just pray and praise and work.

Experience 16. Learning to Trust
(Chapter 27)

It was in the meetings (I spoke about earlier) that I learned to trust. The Lord spoke to me to trust Him when He said to do something.

The preacher had asked for pledges for the missionary, and the Lord spoke to me to answer the call.

I argued and said that I didn't have any money.

The Holy Spirit still tugged at me, and I just kept telling the Lord that I didn't have any money.

Well, after the service and all the way home and the next morning, I felt the Lord was very grieved with me. I got down to pray, and I just couldn't seem to get in touch with the Lord. I felt just terrible.

I got in the car to see my lady-preacher friend, and I began to tell her what had happened and how I felt the Lord was so grieved with me.

She said, "The Lord wouldn't leave you just for that."

I didn't feel any better; I felt the same.

Later on, as I went home, the phone rang, and it was my father. He wanted to know if I would come and help him with his work, and I said I would.

After several hours, I had some money, and then I could see why the Lord had said to give, as He knew that I would have some money. That taught me a good lesson about doing as the Lord says.

Experience 17. Another Healing
(Chapter 28)

Just a few weeks later, I arrived at the church early, as I was so anxious to get there and pray before the service started.

The pastor came up to me and asked me to play the piano for the evening service.

I said I couldn't play their songs, as they were so different from the way they sang in the church I had come out of.

He just kept at me, and though I protested much, he didn't give in. So finally, I consented to try. It just happened that the first song was one that I knew, and so I played it.

Then, the pastor stepped up and said, "People, God wants to do something here tonight. If you need anything from God, you just come up to the altar."

I just sat there and thought, "Wow, I don't need anything from God. He has saved me and solved my problems, and He has healed me and so I don't need anything." I thought I would just sit there and pray for the different ones that needed prayer; when all at once, I felt someone come around behind me. (I had my eyes close.) They put their hands on my eyes behind my glasses. I had forgotten that I wore glasses. The pastor prayed, "Lord, heal these eyes," and he walked away.

I thought, "Why, I hadn't even asked for prayer, and I was the first one he had prayed for."

I opened my eyes and saw that he was praying for others, and no one was even looking at me. My glasses were all smudged from his fingers, so I took them off, as I couldn't see through them. I looked at the song book to see what I could see. Without my glasses (before this), the sentences would always run together, and they were impossible to read.

As I looked at the song book, the sentences were all clear, and each word was separate and as clear as a bell.

I thought again, "If this is faith, I don't feel anything." I had the idea that you had to get a shock or be knocked off your chair or something unusual happened when you got healed.

Experience 18. Fear
(Chapter 29)

January 1966

I had only been saved for a short time, and everything seemed wonderful. My husband had not accused me anymore since I was born again, as he acted like he was afraid of me.

Well, this particular night, we had gone to bed, and I was nearly asleep when he began to say mean things and accuse me of sexual acts with men.

He went on for a while, and finally I said, "I'm not going to listen to any more of this talk. I've never done any of those things that you are accusing me of, so just stop talking that way!"

He got quiet, and eventually I went to sleep.

During the night and in the darkness, I awoke to the feeling that someone was sitting on my feet and ankles. I was lying on my left side, and my right ankle was on top of my left one. I tried to move my feet, but the weight was too heavy. My husband was asleep beside me. I was gripped with fear. I knew if I screamed, my husband would wake up and react, maybe by killing me. There was such an evil feeling in the room. I just lay there, my heart pounding, and I ached all over from being so tense. It seemed like a long time, and the weight on my feet began to slowly lift as if whoever was sitting on my feet started to raise up. I guess you know I didn't sleep anymore that night. I just kept saying in my mind and spirit, "Jesus, Jesus, Jesus."

When I got up in the morning, I was still overwhelmed with that fear. It stayed with me all day. I'd never experienced anything like that before, and being a new Christian, I didn't know what to do about it. I thought, "I'm afraid to go to bed tonight; maybe it will happen again."

It was a Wednesday night, so I went to church that evening. When I arrived, I did what most of us did, and that was to gather around the altar, kneeling and praying. I couldn't even pray. All I could think of was what had happened during the night before, and I kept crying. I finally got up and went and sat down in a seat, still crying.

The pastor was going to start the Bible study when he said, "What's the matter, Sister Donna?"

I stood to my feet, still crying, and told him what I had experienced, and he asked me to come and stand in front of him in the center aisle for prayer. He laid hands on me and commanded that spirit of fear to leave.

I fell on the floor and lay there in perfect peace. I could hear him talking, and when someone laughed, he said, "Don't laugh! That fear was real."

I never again experienced anything like that. I also learned how to deal with the spirit of fear. I found the Scripture in 2 Timothy 1:7, where it says, "For God has not given us the spirit of fear; but of power, and of love and of a sound mind."

Experience 19. My Father's Trial of Health
(Chapter 30)

February 1966

"The doctor is going to admit me to the hospital, and he is going to operate on me in a few days," my dad was speaking to me in a firm, quiet manner.

I was shocked, to say the least. I didn't know that he had anything wrong with him, or had been seeing a doctor.

As I looked into his face, I could see the worry and fear that I hadn't noticed before.

At his point, he began to confide in me. He shared how he had been having some physical problems and had gone to see his doctor.

After an examination, the doctor gave him the results: The trouble was his prostate gland, and the doctor felt that it could be corrected with surgery. They had made a date for Dad to enter the hospital. This is the reason he was telling me now, as he would be admitted in a few days, and he couldn't keep it secret any longer.

"Well, Pa, it's up to you, whatever you want to do," I replied, visibly shaken. I told him that I thought everything would be all right, as he had a good doctor; and he would have the best surgeon to operate.

Three days later, after my dad had been admitted to the hospital, his doctor stopped me in the hall as I was walking to his room.

"Donna, I'd like to talk to you," he said.

He looked worried and acted like he didn't want to say the things that he had to tell me.

"Your dad is in very serious condition. We have found out that his heart is a lot worse than we thought it was, and his age of 81 is against him too. This is the reason we haven't operated already. We don't know if his heart could stand the operation." The doctor continued, "I have talked with the specialist, and we have decided to go ahead and operate and see what we find; but it doesn't look good."

I just stood there looking at him in disbelief. I had no idea that my dad had all these problems. I didn't know what to do, so I told him to do whatever my dad wanted. If they still felt they should operate, then go ahead, whatever they felt was best for him.

The doctor operated the next day, and I stayed there with my dad as much as possible. The nurse came in every few hours with an injection for pain. This was the first time my dad had been in a hospital or had surgery. He was pretty miserable later, but the doctor told him he could have something for pain when he needed it.

A couple of days later, the doctor called me and said, "I felt you should know what we found when we operated on your dad. We found that he was full of cancer, and so we just sewed him back up. There wasn't anything we could do, but his heart is so bad that he will probably go with that first."

I said, "You haven't told him yet, have you? Mom always said that when Dad had anything seriously wrong with him, he would just give up."

The doctor said, "The surgeon is going to tell him this morning; he probably already knows by now."

"Give me the doctor's phone number, and I will call him and see," I said.

He gave me the phone number, and I quickly called the surgeon. He told me that he had already told him, and it didn't seem to upset him.

I rushed right up to the hospital and hurried to my dad's room. His bed was empty. I quickly went over to Mr. Smith in the other bed and asked him if he knew where my dad was. He told me he was in the bathroom.

Very quietly, I asked him if he noticed how my dad acted when the doctor told him he had cancer.

He looked at me with a surprised look and said, "Is that what he was trying to tell him? I didn't understand him to mean that, and I don't think your dad knows that he has cancer."

Just then, my dad came out of the bathroom and went over and got back into bed.

I walked over and greeted him and asked him how he was feeling. He said that he didn't feel too bad. We talked for quite a while, but I didn't tell him that he had cancer. I'd keep that information from him as long as possible, and I would tell others not to tell him either.

The next afternoon, before I entered his hospital room, I could hear my father moaning, and I hurried to his bedside. I asked him what was the matter, and he answered that he was in such terrible pain that he could hardly stand it.

"I'll go and get the nurse to come and give you a shot for pain," I said.

She pulled his chart and looked at it. She said, "It says here that your father just had something an hour ago, so it will be three hours before he gets another shot for pain."

I told her that the doctor had said that he could have a shot whenever he needed it.

She said that was through yesterday; but today, it would be only every four hours.

What was I to do? Then the nurse said that she would tell him, and she spoke to him on the intercom, "It will be a few hours before your next shot, Mr. Storey."

I walked back into his room wondering what I could do to help him. He would have to suffer with the pain for at least three hours. I thought I could pray for him, but I had only been saved a few months, and I sort of felt that the preacher should pray for him. As I stood by his bed, I thought that this wasn't just an earache (ear-ache): This was cancer, and a lot of pain.

I said, "Let me rub your back. Maybe that will help you relax." I began to rub his back, and I fervently prayed silently, "Oh Lord, please do something. Put him to sleep or something, but help him."

It seemed that, instantly, my father went to sleep, and then I walked over by the window and sat down on the chair that was there. I talked to my dad's roommate for quite a while. He was a Christian, and so he was telling me about his experiences serving the Lord.

Suddenly, my dad woke up. He said, "Donna, what did you do?"

I thought maybe I was talking too loud and woke him up. I told him that I hadn't done anything; I was talking to his roommate.

He said, "Oh yes, you did something. When you touched my back, what did you do? I felt something, and all the pain went away."

I jumped up and began to praise the Lord. I said the Lord must have done it, as I had quietly prayed that the Lord would take away the pain. The room-mate began to laugh and said, "Hey! We should keep her here; she's better than all the pills and shots they have here."

In just a few days, he was discharged, and I took him to my home to recuperate, as he lived alone; but he wasn't healed.

Experience 20. My Father's Trial of Faith
(Chapter 31)

March 1966

Pa stayed for a couple of weeks, but he wasn't too happy. He wanted to go home, so he asked me if he could go home for a few hours. He said that he would come right back, so I said he could go.

He was gone quite a while, so I called him on the phone and asked him if anything was wrong, as he hadn't come back. He told me he wasn't coming back. He was staying home. He had made up his mind, so he stayed by himself for the next few months.

One afternoon, he drove out to my home and sat down at the kitchen table. I could see that his condition had deteriorated so much in the last few days.

While he had been in the hospital, I had visited with his room-mate's wife when they had been sleeping; and she had given me some magazines from a Christian organization. Being a new Christian, I read them hungrily, and I had been reading one that day Dad had come out.

I began to tell him about the man I had been reading about. The man had been dying, and God had healed him and gave him the gift of praying for others; and they were healed and he preaches.

"I wish I could go where he is so he could pray for me, and I could be healed. I am so sick," he said as he looked at me and I began to smile.

"Pa, that man is going to be just a few miles from here tonight, and I am going to take a group of ladies to go hear him. Would you like to go to?" I asked.

"Oh, could I?" he said with his eyes begging.

"Of course, if you don't mind riding with a bunch of ladies," I laughed.

That evening, when we got to the meeting, all the seats in the lower level were filled, and the bleachers were filling very quickly. We hurried to find ourselves a seat. We had to sit up four rows in the bleachers.

Shortly after we were seated, the music began and the meeting was on. The minister came out and began to sing. Then he started to call out different people and tell them their needs. As they responded, he would pray for them and they would be healed. We were all thrilled at the mighty things that God was doing for these people.

The meeting changed, and the minister said, "Now folks, we are going to take the offering. God says that, tonight, you are to only give one dollar, no more and no less."

My dad jumped up, pulled out his billfold and took out a dollar bill. He ran down the steps of the bleachers and onto the main floor. Running up to the minister, he held his dollar bill out to him and said, "Here's my dollar bill. Now will you pray for me?" Pa wanted to be healed now.

The minister looked down at him and softly said to him, "Brother, we're going to take the offering now, but I will pray for you later."

Dejectedly, Pa turned around and slowly walked back to the little gate to the bleachers. He pushed it open and went just inside and sat down there. He didn't come back to the seat he had sat in before.

The meeting went on and the preacher spoke for a while. Then he said there would be a prayer line.

The people began to run to get into the line. Those in wheelchairs were first. He prayed a longer prayer for those in the front of the line, and by the time he got to my dad, he just put his hand on his head and said, "Give him what he needs, Lord." Then he went on to the next person.

Dad shuffled back to where I was sitting. He looked at me and said, "That didn't do any good. I didn't feel anything."

"Who said that you had to feel anything? I never felt anything when I was healed," I said.

We stayed a while longer, as some of the ladies that had come with us went for prayer.

Dad grumbled all the way home. When we got to his house, I got out of the car and walked up to his door with him. He was still complaining that it was just a waste of time going, as it didn't do any good.

I looked at him and told him, "You had so much faith in that man tonight. If you would just direct that faith up to God and ask Him to heal you right now, He would do it. Man can't heal us: Only God can do any of these things for us."

He turned and went into his house, still fussing.

The next morning, the phone rang, and it was my dad. He began to tell me how well he felt.

I began to laugh and tell him, "You must have asked God to heal you. You are not the same dad I left last night."

Praise God, we don't have to depend on people to heal us or meet any of our needs that we have. If we just have faith the size of a mustard seed, we can move mountains. Let's be sure we direct our faith in the right direction.

Experience 21. The Refrigerator
(Chapter 32)

"The trial of your faith is more precious than fine gold," so the Scripture says. But sometimes we don't realize that we are being tested.

As had become my habit, I heard the alarm go off at 5:30 a.m. and quickly turned it off so as not to wake the rest of my family. This was the time I always spent in prayer and Bible-reading and waiting on the Lord. This was the best time of the day, as I was free and not bogged down with phone calls and noise yet. The time spent there was so necessary for me to learn of and lean on my Lord Jesus. Then, at 7:00, the activity really began, as everyone was preparing for the day before them of both school and work.

As I busied myself preparing the breakfast, I noticed that, as I opened the refrigerator door, there was water standing in the bottom and dripping out of the freezer compartment. I checked the dial to see if someone had accidentally turned it off, but it was turned on.

I quickly got breakfast over with and everyone on their way for the day.

I got out the book telling about the refrigerator and began trying all the different things that it said to check, but it was to no avail.

I began the mopping-up operation, still wondering what could be the matter with the refrigerator. I thought, "Well, I guess I'd better call the repairman and have him come and take a look at it.

A lady answered the phone when I called, and I told her my problem. She said that she would have the man come out later in the day, as he was all booked up for hours.

As there was nothing else I could do, I got busy and started washing. Every time I walked past the refrigerator, I'd check it over again: It was still not running.

Several hours passed by, and I happened to think. . . "Why did I call the repairman? I don't have any money to pay for a house-call, and didn't my Lord say that He was an ever-present help in the time of need?"

I walked over to the refrigerator and laid both my hands on it and said, "In the name of Jesus, I command you to run." Nothing happened: Just silence.

Then, I went to the telephone and dialed the repairman's number again. The same lady answered again, and I told her that I was cancelling my repair call.

She wanted to know why, so I just told her that it was okay now.

I walked away from the phone and listened to hear the refrigerator hum: There was none. I just said, "Thank you, Jesus, for fixing my refrigerator for me," and went on about my daily chores.

Several hours went by, and I completely forgot all about the problem. I have learned, over the years, to take your burdens to the Lord and leave them there.

While putting some dish towels away later, I became aware of the steady hum of the refrigerator and found, looking inside, that it was functioning properly. *Praise the Lord*, there is no problem too big or too small for my Jesus.

Experience 22. The Voice Speaks Again
(Chapter 33)

While praying one morning for the Lord's direction for my day, I felt the Lord telling me to quit my job working for my father on that day, and go to a small factory and put my application in there, as I was to be working there beginning the next day.

I went off to work for my father that morning. When I felt the time was right, I went to my father and told him that I had to quit my job with him that day, as I had told Jesus that I would do anything that He told me to do, and this is what He had hold me that morning.

My father looked at me like he was studying me, and then he said, "Well, if that's what you have to do, then you can leave at noon."

At noon, I left work and drove over to the small factory that the Lord had directed me to go to. I went inside and told the receptionist I wanted an application for employment.

She handed it to me, and I went over and sat down at a nearby desk. After filling out the application, I returned it to the receptionist.

She looked it over and then looked back to me. She said, "Neither the boss or his son are here right now, but if you could wait a few minutes, the son would be back. He has gone to the Post Office."

I told her that I could wait, so I sat down; and in just a few minutes, the son returned.

The receptionist told him why I was there and handed him my employment application.

He looked at me and looked at the application, and motioned for me to follow him into his office. He kept looking at me very perplexed. Finally, he said, "Are you clairvoyant?"

I didn't know what he was talking about. I just said, "No."

He said he couldn't understand what was going on: He had just returned from placing an ad in the newspaper for two women to come to work; and when he got back to the factory, I was waiting to see him about a job.

We talked for a while and then he said he liked my application, and he would talk to his father about me. He said his father would be back in a few hours, and then he would call me.

As I stood up to leave, I asked him what the women wore to work.

He told me, and as I started out the door, I turned to him and said, "I'll probably see you in the morning."

Shortly after arriving at home, the phone rang. It was the son calling me to tell me that his father said to hire me. And he asked if I could be at work at 8:00 a.m.

I told him I would be happy to come to work that next morning.

The next morning, I walked into the factory, and the receptionist told me where to go to the locker room.

As I opened the door, I came face-to-face with six women. They all looked at me, and one of them said, "Who are you?"

I told them Mr. Smith had hired me the day before. I was to start working with them, and a woman named "Ann" was to show me what to do.

Ann stepped forward and held out her hand for me to shake. As I shook her hand, she told me her name, and I realized that she was the mother of a boy that my son had attended school with. She led me over to the workbench where we would be working.

We were talking about our children, and the lady who did the shipping for the firm came by our area. She stopped and asked Ann if she had an aspirin, as she had a terrible headache.

Ann told her that she had aspirin in her purse in the locker and told her to go get some. After she had walked away, Ann looked over at me and asked me what I took for headaches.

I just smiled and didn't say anything.

Then, Ann said, "You don't take anything, do you?"

I told her that I used prayer.

Ann laughed and said, "I thought so."

She began to ask me other questions, and then I realized that she was the one that the Lord had sent me there to minister to. I hadn't come to just work for a man, but to work for the Lord.

The very first day, she began to tell me the things that were on her heart: How her husband had died recently and problems with her children.

I just sympathized with her and let the Lord lead me in what to say.

We talked every day all day. She was soaking it all up like a big sponge. Within three months, she had all her problems taken care of, as Jesus was teaching her how to trust Him. Ann had turned her life over to Jesus and was letting Him lead her in her new life.

Shortly after that, Ann was transferred to a different area in the plant, and I only saw her coming-and-going into work and leaving. It was then I realized my job there was finished.

The next thing was how I was going to tell my boss that I was leaving there. I told the Lord that I would just go to him and tell him that the Lord had sent me there to work, and now the Lord was telling me to leave.

The Lord said not to go to him. He said not to cast my pearls before the swine: He wouldn't understand. So I waited to see how I would go about leaving.

The next morning, as I walked into work, I became very ill. I felt so sick all that day, and I couldn't imagine why.

Later in the day, when I walked out the door of the plant, I noticed that I felt okay. "Very strange," I thought.

When I arrived at work the next morning, I was feeling great. But in just a few minutes after I started work, I got that sick feeling again. I said, "Lord, what's going on?"

He said, "You needed an excuse to leave your job, so I'm giving you one."

Armed with my excuse, I headed for the boss.

He got very upset when I told him that I wanted to quit.

When he asked me why, I just told him that I was sick.

He looked at me for a few seconds and then said, "Take two weeks off from work and then you'll feel better."

I told him, "No, I have to quit."

He said he'd think about it.

I went back to work. I felt so weak I could hardly stand, and finally he came over to me and said I could quit.

When I walked out the door, I was fine again.

Once again, the Lord had made a way for me out of another situation. *Praise God*! The Lord had given me this job for three months, just so I could minister to one dear lady.

Experience 23. God's Power at Work
(Chapter34)

It was a cold, crisp, winter-like night. An icy wind was blowing, and tomorrow would be Thanksgiving Day. We were hurrying to church for a Thanksgiving service. We usually held these in our own little church, but it was decided that several churches would gather together for a combined service.

My two youngest children, Melanie and Kevin, were with me, as they were going to spend the evening with their sister. I had driven a few more miles to pick up our friend Sister Fountain, who always rode with me.

We soon arrived at Terry's, my oldest daughter. I watched the kids hop out of the car and go into the house, and I drove on to the church.

The church felt warm and cozy as we entered and greeted others. We quickly found a seat and got settled in. The music was wonderful, and we all sang heartily.

After a few minutes, Sister Hazel slipped in and sat down beside us. She usually rode with us, but recently, her husband told her that she was to drive alone. So she came by herself.

The pastors took turns peaching, and then they asked everyone to gather around the front for a time of prayer before closing the service.

After a time of prayer, I started back to my seat. Hazel got there before me and was sitting there putting on her coat when she just began to slide over to her left and lay there on the seat. Her face was looking up, and I looked down at her. Her eyes were wide open, and they were rolled back so I could only see the whites of her eyes.

I said, "Hazel, you look just like my mom when I found her dead."

Sister Fountain came up beside me and asked me what was wrong.

I said, "It's Hazel; I think she is dead."

Sister Fountain sat down beside Hazel and began to rub Hazel's wrist.

I remembered how Sister Fountain had told me that, if I should die before her, she wouldn't come to my funeral, as she didn't like to be around dead people. But here she was, rubbing Hazel's arm.

About that time, I noticed Sister Horning standing behind Hazel, bending over putting on her coat; and when she looked down and saw Hazel lying there, she grabbed her by the head and pulled her up into a sitting position and fervently began to pray for her. And after a few minutes, Hazel began to move a little.

My pastor walked up beside me and asked me what had happened.

I told him Hazel was just sitting there and she fell over onto the seat.

He said she probably just fainted, and he walked around the end of the pew and told Sister Horning that he'd take over.

By this time, Hazel was moving and began to put her coat on.

I watched Hazel, and she seemed very confused. She gathered up her things and headed for the door.

I went over to her and asked her if she was all right.

She said she was, so I asked her what happened to her, and she said, "All I know is I was as cold as death; cold as death." She turned and walked out the door, very slowly.

I went to my pastor and told him that Hazel wasn't acting normal.

He just laughed and said she'd be all right.

I thought I'd better follow her and make sure she got home all right. If anything should happen to her on the way home, her husband might stop her from going to church. Sister Fountain and I hurried to my car and watched her start her car and move very slowly down the street in the direction of her mother's.

As she was driving so slowly, I knew I had time to go and pick up my kids and get back to her mother's driveway.

Her car was still there, and she was still seated in it. She never got out. After sitting there for a few minutes, she slowly backed her car out onto the street. She headed in the direction she would take to get to the freeway.

I stayed close behind her, and she drove very slowly, not going over 35 miles per hour. I followed her until she drove into her driveway. She turned in, and I followed her right up to her garage. She drove up to the garage and got out and went inside her home. She didn't know I had parked right beside her.

I waited a few minutes and then I drove on to take Sister Fountain home. As we drove on, we discussed what had happened that night. We agreed that Hazel had died and God had raised her back to life, but we were perplexed, as we had never heard of anything like this happening . . . except in the Bible.

When we arrived at Sister Fountain's house, I used her phone and called Hazel. When I asked her if she was all right, she said she was preparing her turkey for roasting the next day. I told her I would call her the next day. I drove home puzzling over the events that had happened that night.

Waiting till I thought everyone had finished their Thanksgiving dinner, I called Hazel again, asking her how she was and what had happened the night before.

She just kept repeating over and over, "All I know is I was as cold as death, . . . cold as death."

Not getting any answers from her, I called Sister Horning. When she answered the phone, I just came right out and asked her, "What happened last night?"

She answered me with a question, "What do you think happened?"

I said, "Hazel died."

Then she began to tell me what had happened to her the morning before:

She had been baking and preparing for her Thanksgiving dinner the next day when the phone rang. A dear Christian lady was on the line and said that God had told her she should call her and tell her to pray.

She told her she had prayed.

Her friend said, "God said to tell you to pray again."

She told her as soon as she turned off the oven she would pray.

After taking her baking out of the oven, she went into the bedroom and knelt down and began to pray again. She didn't know what to pray about, so she just prayed for everyone and everything she had prayed for before. After that, she just waited on the Lord.

As she knelt there, she began to have a vision:

It was like she was high above a church service, looking down; and she saw the death angel hovering above the people, ready to touch someone.

The vision ended and she got up, wondering what that was all about. Was someone going to die?

She went on to say that, when her brother came to pick her up for church service, she told him what had happened that morning and the vision. She said, after she got to church, she forgot all about it until she was leaning over the pew and saw Hazel lying there. That's when she began to pray for her.

As I began to put this together, I could see what the Lord had been doing. Why didn't the others see that Hazel had died? Why had God allowed me to see this miracle?

This all happened on Wednesday night, and the questions were still running through my mind on Sunday morning as I was sitting in church. As different ones gave their testimonies, I just sat there saying nothing. I thought, if I said anything about Hazel and what I had seen, they would think I was crazy.

The preacher began to preach; and as I sat there, the Lord began to tell me that I was just like Peter: denying Him.

I said, "No, I'm not, Lord. I never denied You."

He said, "Yes, you have. You've denied me."

I repeated that I hadn't denied Him.

Then He said, "You saw a miracle, and you never even told about it."

I said, "Lord, they were all there, and they all saw it too."

He said, "They didn't see what you saw."

I felt terrible. I said, "All right, Lord, You just make a space for me, and I'll get up and tell them all that happened."

All the time the preacher was preaching, I was hurting under the Lord's words.

At the end of the services, the pastor said, "Are all hearts clear? Does anyone have anything to say?"

I jumped up and shouted, "I've got something to say: Hazel died in the church the other night."

It got very quiet in there, and the pastor said, "Well, Hazel, did you die the other night? Did you see the Lord? To be absent from the body is to be present with the Lord."

Hazel spoke up, "I don't know what happened. All I know is I was as cold as death, cold as death."

Sister Horning jumped up and shouted, "She did die; I know she died."

The silence was so thick in that room you could have cut it with a knife. My face burned with embarrassment. I could tell that they didn't believe me. Standing there, I felt every eye on me.

The pastor said, "Well, Hazel, if you didn't see the Lord, you didn't die."

With that, the pastor closed in prayer, and the people began to gather in little groups talking in whispers.

Looking around, I saw that the pastor's wife and a few other ladies were huddled in a group whispering, and then they would look at me.

I walked over by them and said, "I know you don't believe me, so would you like me to leave the church?"

The pastor's wife patted my arm like she was trying to humor me and said, "No, you don't have to leave the church."

I went over and picked up my things and walked out. No one came to me and said anything.

Sister Fountain and I talked as we drove home. We still agreed that what we had seen was real, whether anyone else believed it or not.

So many strange things had happened to me since I was born again. I wondered if things like this happened to others. My life was really changing. This was all so different than anything I had ever experienced or heard anyone tell about.

Experience 24. Another Mighty Miracle
(Chapter 35)

One evening, Sister Fountain called and asked me if I would like to ride to Detroit with her and some friends to a Full Gospel Businessmen's Breakfast that was being held the next morning. This was the 13th of December, and the weather was very cold.

I thought about it and told her I would be happy to go. Early the next morning, the car (that was to take me) drove into the yard. It was very dark out, as it was only 5:30 a.m.

I ran outside into the cold, brisk wind. Grabbing the door handle, I pulled the back passenger-door open and hurried inside. The warmth inside the car felt so good after only being outside for just a minute.

The Andersons asked me if I had ever been to a Full Gospel Businessmen's meeting, and I told them, "No." But I had read their little magazine *The Voice*, which was full of wonderful testimonies of men whose lives God had changed.

On the way to Detroit, Sister Fountain and I talked about things that the Lord was doing in our lives. We had no idea what God had in store for us that day.

The meeting was held at a large restaurant; and as we drove into the parking lot, I could see other cars slowing down to turn into the same parking lot.

We hurried into the building and hung up our coats and found a table near the platform where the speakers would be sitting.

As I looked around at the others who were already there, I noticed a young man sitting looking at his Bible. He had a big white handkerchief; and after he would read something from the Bible, he would put the handkerchief over his face and sob.

I just couldn't take my eyes off this man. He was so humble, and I wondered what he was reading that touched him so.

As the room filled to capacity, I kept watching this man out of the corner of my eye. The leader prayed over the food and everyone began eating, everyone except this man. Others sat at the table with him, and by this time, he had stopped crying; but I noticed that he wasn't eating any breakfast.

When the breakfast was finished and dishes were cleared away, the meeting began with lots of hearty singing. I was touched by the love that I felt in that place.

The president took care of the formalities and then he said, "I see Brother Bogel out there. Would you come up here, Brother Bogel?"

I looked around to see who he was talking to, and it was the man who had been crying. When I heard the name "Brother Bogel," I thought, "That's the man we listen to on the radio that prays for people who phone in their prayer requests."

He walked up to the platform, and they asked him to say something. He spoke in a very soft voice. He told us that, when he was finishing up his broadcast early that morning around 2:00 a.m., the Lord told him that he was to come to the breakfast that morning. He didn't know why, as he had been the speaker at a previous meeting. The Lord had gently insisted, so he came. He told us that he didn't know why he was there, but he was just being obedient.

The president asked him to stay up on the platform, so he took a seat up there.

The main speaker was a young dentist. As he spoke, it was very quiet, as what he was saying was so interesting.

All of a sudden, off to my right, I heard this sound of someone making a gurgling noise in their throat. I looked over at the next table and saw this woman sitting there with her head tipped back over the back of the chair, and I could look right into her face. She was only about six feet from me. It was just like what had happened at the church two weeks before with Hazel. Her eyes were rolled back so all you could see was the whites, and her mouth was open and she wasn't breathing.

It got very quiet in there, and one of the ladies at that table began to shake her and say, "What's the matter, Dear?" Then she looked up at the men on the platform and said, "I think you need to pray for her; I think she's sick."

With that, several of the men came down off the platform and gathered around her and very quietly began to pray.

I began to cry and leaned over to Sister fountain and said, "Everywhere we go, they die." I kept thinking, "Why don't they pray with authority? Don't they know the lady is dead?"

I looked up at the platform and I saw only Brother Bogel sitting there. I began to pray that God would tell Brother Bogel to get down there and pray. I knew that he would pray with authority; and just about that time, he jumped up and hurried down there and grabbed that lady by the head and began to rebuke Satan. In just a few minutes, that lady began to move and God restored her.

The men went back up to the platform and the meeting resumed.

I could hardly wait for the meeting to get over so I could go speak to Brother Bogel. When I finally got close enough to speak to him, I asked him, "Brother Bogel, what happened to that lady?"

He answered me with the question, "What do you think happened?"

I told him that the lady had died, and he just began to praise the Lord. Then I told him about Hazel dying in the church just two weeks before. We both agreed that it was the Lord doing all this.

On the ride back home later that day, Sister Anderson looked around at us in the back seat and said, "Isn't that something about that lady fainting during the meeting?"

Sister Fountain and I just looked at each other.

I was a little afraid to go to meetings after that, as I didn't know if it was my fault that these two ladies had died or not.

I guess you know that I testified about this happening in Detroit. I just told the folks that they didn't have to believe me, but I was going to tell it anyhow. I think some of the folks thought that I was kind of weird, but I didn't care what people thought as long as I pleased the Lord.

Why did the Lord choose to let Sister Fountain and me see these things, and others that were there didn't see the same thing? I was to find out several years later. The Lord was preparing me to pray for people that died in a service.

Experience 25. Be Sure Your Sins Will Find You Out
(Chapter 36)

"How did you know that, Mom?" My children often asked this question of me. They thought it was just me knowing these things, but the Holy Spirit would drop a clue into my thoughts; and when I would go and follow up the so-called intuitions, I'd find out things that I would have no way of knowing.

Such was the morning in September when I was busying myself doing some repair work in our utility room.

It was such a lovely sunny day; I felt like working.

I decided I'd finish closing in the chimney and make the room look a little neater. I stood looking at the chimney blocks for a few minutes, studying them; and then decided what I would attempt to do.

I started going through the boards and other materials that I had on hand. I chose a piece of material and took it back to the utility room with me.

I thought to myself, "I'll need some cement nails, hammer, square, and a pencil."

As I began to get the tools together, I realized that the hammer was missing from the place where I usually kept it. I tried to remember: Had I used it and forgot to put it back? Then I recalled that my husband had taken it with him to his work a few days before that, and it must still be there.

As I started to leave the room to go to the telephone, the Lord spoke to me, "Donna, if you will go out into the woods behind your property, you will find something."

Walk back to that big hole? A little shiver went through me as I began to recall the strange things that had been happening the last few days:

On the previous Saturday afternoon, I and my two daughters had attended the wedding of a friend of ours. When we arrived home from the wedding reception, Kevin ran out to the car to meet us. He shouted excitedly, "You missed all the excitement: The sheriff and police cars and the newspaper photographers and reporters were out at the state property behind our land. Mom, they found a car buried back there!"

I looked at him in wonder and asked him, "Why would anyone want to bury a car? Why didn't they just take it to the junk yard?"

"Mom, it wasn't a junk car; it was a newer one: A Corvette," he said breathlessly.

I really couldn't make much sense of all this conversation.

He went on to tell us all that had happened.

The property, acres-and-acres, was owned by the state; and it was all woods and pine trees. The deer roamed freely back there. The conservation workers would go back there by a road that curved in-and-out through the trees. They planted corn in the clearings. It was left there, and the deer would feed off it in the wintertime.

Kevin went on to tell us that he had seen the sheriff cars turn back onto that road, and so the neighbors followed along to see what they were doing back there. Kevin went along too.

He said that the sheriff had brought along some trustees (prisoners of honor) from the local jail, and they began to dig with shovels. The spot they were working on was a large pile of sand that had been dug up by someone else earlier.

After they had been digging a short time, one of the shovels struck something hard. Everyone ran to the spot to see what he had hit. They began to uncover a full-sized car that was upside-down. They finally finished uncovering it and then had a wrecker lift it out of the hole.

The deputy called in on his radio, and they verified that it was a stolen car that they had been looking for.

Flashbulbs popped and people posed for pictures for the local newspaper, and then they hauled it all away and everyone left the area.

The next day, there was a big picture of the discovery in the paper, along with the headline, "Big Dick Tracy Mystery!"

This was one of the biggest stories for the newspaper in a long, long time.

There were many questions in the minds of the people.

A neighbor girl and her friends had gone horseback riding along the road on the state property, and they saw the pile of sand and some wheels lying on top. They called the sheriff to investigate.

Kevin was still so breathless, as he was trying to fill us in on all the happenings of the afternoon.

We went into the house and I began to prepare supper. I still kept thinking about all that had transpired. Why would anyone want to bury a car? The question was buzzing around in my mind.

Meanwhile, the kids were on the telephone, telling their friends everywhere, what had been happening.

The front door opened, and Bill and a friend came in. I walked over where they were and asked them excitedly, "Did you hear what happened? They found a car buried out in the state property in back of our place!"

They seemed unmoved by it all and just looked back at me and said, "Yah, we heard," and walked away.

It was two days later when the Lord began to speak to me to go back to the hole in the woods.

I started to protest to the Lord, "Lord, You know that I get all mixed up when I go back in the woods: My directions get all fouled up and I'll get lost. I'll be back there all day, lost."

He replied, "Donna, didn't you tell me that you would do anything I asked you to do?"

I tried to change His mind, "Well, yes Lord, but You know I'll probably get all mixed up."

He just kept telling me that I would find something back there, and so I thought to myself, "He always tells me right, so I'd better go back there."

I started to walk through the woods. The underbrush was thick, and I had to press my way through it.

It was very warm walking back there in all that brush; and here-and-there, a spider was busy spinning webs and tying branches-and-leaves together. I brushed it aside and pressed on, looking back toward our house and hoping that I wouldn't get my directions all mixed up.

The wild blackberry bushes reached out and pulled at my clothes as the birds flitted overhead and under the bushes.

After what seemed like a very long time, I broke out of the woods. Here was the road that the kids had told me was back there. I thought, "If I keep on this road, maybe I won't get lost." I began walking along the sandy road in the direction I thought I should go. In just a few minutes, I could see a large pile of sand and knew that this must be the place.

When I walked over to that gaping hole, it was scary. It reminded me of an over-sized grave. I looked around and didn't see anything unusual. I questioned, "Lord, what am I looking for?"

No response.

I asked myself, "How can I cover all the area around here and not miss anything?"

Then, an idea began to form in my mind: If I start walking around in a circle and just keep making the circle smaller each time I walk around, then maybe I'll find what I am looking for.

I began to walk around and around and around. I didn't see anything at all, except for a few little "springs." It seems the engine had been taken out of the car back there, and these were some of the springs from that.

I came to the big tree where the chain-fall had been hung to lift the engine out, and then . . . I noticed something behind the tree. I saw what looked like a piece of cloth. I ran across there and picked up this cloth: It was a shirt. I held it up and began to check it over. The label was still in the back of the neckline, and I held it closer to read it: *Penny's*!

This was Bill's shirt. I had just bought it for him a few weeks before this. I felt like someone had hit me in the stomach. "Oh no, Lord," I wailed, "Don't tell me that my Bill is mixed up in this car mess." I knew then why the Lord had me come back to the hole and look for something.

Bill had been rebellious for several years. He felt that he was a big man and was running around with several fellows older than he was, and some younger boys too. As I hurried back through the woods, I was both hurt and angry. I was glad the Lord had told me

102

about this, but I was wishing it hadn't ever happened. Now, what do I do?

When I got back to the house, I walked in and went right to Bill's bedroom. Bill was lying there asleep. I walked over to his bed and said, "Get up, Bill. I want to know what you know about that car that was buried out there in the state property."

He opened his eyes with surprise written all over his face. He looked at me and said, "What do you want?"

I told him that I had been out to the hole and found his shirt there. I wanted to know what he knew about it.

He just ignored my questioning and said, "Get out of here and leave me alone."

I said I wasn't leaving until I found out what he knew about all that had happened, "You were in on that whole thing, weren't you Bill?"

He just kept on angrily shouting, "Get out of here and leave me alone!"

I turned and left the room, and in a few minutes, he came out. He looked at me with much contempt in his eyes and said, "What do you think you're gonna do?"

I said, "You're going to go down to the police and tell them all you know about that car business."

He looked at me like I had lost my mind and shouted back at me, "I'm not going anyplace; you can't pin this on me; I didn't do anything."

I could tell by looking at his face that he was lying.

He turned away from me and went to the telephone. He began to dial a number.

I stood there wondering what I should do next.

He began to speak to his friend, and I overheard him talking about going to California.

I said, "You're not going to California; you are going to stay right here and face the music.

He retorted, "That's what you think!"

I got the car keys and walked out and got into the car and drove over to my husband's business a couple of miles away. I related to him what had been happening at home.

He just stood there looking at me, in shock, like I was telling him some strange story about someone else. When he finally came to himself, he said, "Well, what are we going to do?"

I said, "Listen, he thinks he's a big man, and if we don't stop him now, he's liable to get a gun somewhere and do some of the dumb things that he sees on TV. He'll get himself killed. We've got to turn him in for his own good."

I hurried home, and when I got there, Bill was gone.

I thought, "Oh dear God, don't let him go to California with this other boy and his uncle."

My husband went looking for him, and later that evening, found him at the apartment of one of his older friends. He persuaded Bill to go down to the police department, and when they began to question him about the car theft and everything that had followed, Bill decided to be like the guys on TV: He told them that he had stolen the car all by himself, had taken it to the state property, and had taken the engine out by himself. Of course, he turned the car over into the hole that he had dug and gotten rid of the engine too. He wasn't going to be any squealer.

The officers knew he wasn't telling the truth, and so after they had taken all the report down, they let him come home with his dad until the next morning. Then I would have to take him back to the police department to await what they would decide to do.

They already had a line on the other boys involved, and they were looking for them. Several of the fellows involved were never arrested, but Bill was sentenced later and given 5-years-probation and 1 year at correctional camp, plus restitution and court costs.

After I became a born-again Christian, I had been fervently praying that the Lord would save all my children too. While all of this was taking place with Bill, I cried all the more to the Lord.

One evening at church, while Bill was awaiting sentencing and was allowed to stay at home, I went down to the altar and implored the Lord with much tears and pleading to save Bill at any cost.

People, we don't really realize what we pray sometimes: I had said, "Save him at any cost." Well, God heard that prayer from my heart.

Two months had passed since the discovery of the buried car. The ground was covered with snow, and the kids were off one afternoon tobogganing at a nearby hill.

Bill had stayed at home. A car drove in and deposited some of our children from the hill. They said, when they came in, "Hey Bill, somebody out in that car wants to see you."

Not even taking his coat, Bill ran out and got into the car with the fellows. The car drove off and Bill didn't come home that night.

The next day, he didn't come home, and I was very concerned about him. That evening about 4:00 p.m., the court officer stopped by. He came in and asked me if I knew where Bill was.

I told him that I was so worried about him, as he hadn't come home the night before. He hadn't even taken his coat with him.

The court officer looked at me and said, "Don't worry; he's in jail."

I was shocked and was trying not to fall apart. I asked him, "In jail? What has he done now?"

He told of how Bill had gone out and got into that car with those boys. They drove away and had only gone about one-half mile from our home when they stopped the car and pulled out a bottle of wine.

About that time, a patrol car happened to drive by and stopped to investigate this stopped car. The two oldest boys were arrested for contributing to the delinquency of minors. Bill was one of the oldest ones. So, off to jail.

As the court officer was leaving, he turned and said, "Please don't try to get him out this time. At least you will know where he is if he's in jail."

I said, "I guess he will have to stay there, as I haven't any money to get him out."

After he had driven away, I ran to the utility room and fell down on my knees and began to cry out to God, "Oh God, after all that's happened, now why this?"

That still, small vice replied, "Didn't you ask me to save him at any cost?"

"Yes Lord," I replied, "but I didn't think about anything like this happening. I didn't ask You to send him to jail."

He said, "I am starting a work in him, and I am going to save him."

Surprised at His answer, my praises began to fill the room. I jumped up from my knees and ran to the telephone. I dialed a friend, and when she answered, I laughingly shouted, "Hazel, Bill's in jail. *Praise the Lord*! Isn't that wonderful?"

"What?" she answered shocked, "I don't think that is so wonderful."

I began to tell her what had happened and what the Lord had said. I was just thrilled beyond measure. I told her that I wasn't happy that Bill was in jail, but that the Lord had said He was starting a work in him and that He was going to save him.

Bill spent a few days in jail and was released to come home. Two months later, he was sentenced to go to a work correction camp. He was there for six months.

God did really start a work in Bill, and a few years later, he was saved. It seemed like my boys thought they had to go through all the mud-holes on their way to Calvary. It doesn't have to be that way, only if we choose.

Experience 26. Bill Gets a Break and God Keeps Us Safe

(Chapter 37)

After Bill had been at the camp for several months, he called and said he'd been given a weekend to come home.

I called the officials at the camp and got permission to bring him home for a weekend.

My husband didn't have anything to do with anything going on in our family. He just went his own way.

There were five in our family that went, and a friend of Bill's. Bill was waiting for us and was ready to leave.

We started our trip back home. It was a busy weekend with lots of traffic. As I drove along, we heard a "bang," and the car began to sway. Then I realized we had a tire blow on our car.

I just said, "Hang on," and the car spun around in a circle and came to a jarring stop in the median. The traffic just kept flying by.

A trucker came running across the median to our car and asked, "Are you all right? I thought for sure the car would turn over and you would all be dead."

We told him we were all shaken up, but no one was hurt.

He asked who was driving.

I told him I had my hands on the wheel, but the Lord was driving.

The boys changed the tire and I drove us on home.

We talked about what had happened all weekend, thanking the Lord for sparing our lives.

I took Bill back from his weekend off.

A few days later in the newspaper, there was an article where a priest was driving along that same area we'd had the blow-out. He had a blow-out too, but he was killed.

The Bible says, "The devil is out to steal, kill, and destroy; and he doesn't pass up an opportunity."

But, the Bible also says, "The prayers of a righteous man avails much."

Prayer really does changes things.

Experience 27. A New Adventure or Where is Florida, Lord?

(Chapter 38)

It seemed that every time I'd pray, the Lord would say, "Donna, go to Florida."

I'd tell Him, "Lord, I don't want to go to Florida. I don't even know where Florida is."

Finally, after He had told me to go to Florida for several weeks, I said, "Okay, I'll go, but I don't know why I'm going."

It was nearly Christmas.

When I told my husband, he just said, "I don't care where you go."

I told the kids, "If you decide to give me anything for Christmas, just make it money."

I thought that, along with the $20.00 I made cleaning the church (for I had returned to my old church for cleaning it again), we'll have enough money for gas (I thought). Terry had asked her dad Barney if he'd match whatever the kids could raise, and he said "Yes."

Well, Christmas eve, as we had our Christmas, Terry said, "Dad, we've raised $50.00, and you said you'd match it. . . So?"

He just laughed at her and said, "I was just kidding," and he walked out the door.

The kids were pretty upset.

I told them not to worry: If the Lord said to go, He'll see to it that we go.

The next day was Christmas. I and Melanie and Kevin went and cleaned the church. So, with the $50.00 the kids had raised and the $20.00 we got for cleaning the church, we had $70.00.

That afternoon, my dad stopped in on his way home from my brother's. He had gone there to celebrate Christmas with my brother's family.

I sked him if he was ready to go to Florida.

He said, "I thought you were just kidding."

I told him we were leaving in the morning: Melanie, Kevin, and me.

He said, "The only way I'll go is I'll pay for all the gas and motels."

I told him we would pick him up in the morning

The day after Christmas, after my husband left for work, I found a $50.00-bill on the kitchen table.

My husband acted like he was kind of afraid of me after I was born again. He just didn't accuse me anymore and left me alone, no more wild stories about me. We still slept together and lived in the same house, but he went his way and I went mine.

Experience 28. Florida, Here We Come
(Chapter 39)

The kids were ready. Kevin and Melanie had their bags packed and ready to go. We drove downtown to pick up my dad. My dad had to stop at the bank, so we made a quick trip into the grocery store for snacks. We picked up my dad and headed out to the highway. I had a map, so we were sure we could find our way. I'd never driven 100 miles away from home before. "Lead the way, Lord."

We stopped at a motel for the night. As we were all asleep, we felt the ground shaking and a noise that sounded like a train.

I just got up and looked out the back window. Behind our building were railroad tracks level with my eyes, and a huge freight train was rumbling by. In just a little while, along came another train.

My dad was complaining very loudly. He said, "Let's get out of here." We dressed and left there.

We found a restaurant near Chattanooga, Tennessee that was open that early and ordered breakfast. We looked at our plates and said, "What is that blob of white stuff?"

The others, that were there eating, were laughing at us.

When I asked them what that blob of stuff was, they just laughed and didn't say anything. (My sister in Florida would later tell me that it was grits.)

After we ate, we got back on the road. Driving along in Georgia that day, the engine began to make a bad noise. I stopped by the side of the road and found out the water pump quit. I limped along until I found a place to get it fixed. That took $60.00 of our $100.00. Then we went on to Florida.

Experience 29. Florida, Home Sweet Home
(Chapter 40)

We arrived at night, and my sister and brother met us out by the expressway. We followed them into Orlando and my sister's home. Brice's wife (my brother's wife) met me at the door.

She was holding this big Bible and said, "I've got some questions I need you to answer for me."

I told her, "Could it wait until morning? It's late, and I'm very tired."

She said, "Okay."

Some of us stayed at my sister's, and the rest went to my brother's to sleep.

The next day was Sunday, so we all got ready for church. My brother Brice came over to me outside the church and asked me to check out his pastor. *"Help, Lord."*

The pastor and my brother had gone out "Calling" together, and the house they went to had a sick little boy. The parents asked for prayer for him. (Brice had been to a big tent-meeting, and he had seen people healed and delivered from different things.)

When the boy's parents asked for prayer, Brice said. "God can heal him," and he began to pray for him. (The pastor had left and had gone outside and sat in his car.)

After praying for the boy, Brice left. He went out and got into the car.

The pastor was very angry, and he told Brice that God doesn't heal today: Healing was back in the Bible times.

Brice replied, "I just saw people healed a few days ago in this meeting I attended."

The pastor was mad and said he would never go Calling again with Brice.

Brice said the pastor is very cool with him now. He also said, "God healed that boy too."

We went into the church where my Florida family were in the choir. I just sat there praying and listening to the pastor talking.

When the service was over, Brice didn't take off his choir robe. He came hurrying over to me and said, "What did the Lord say?"

I told him, "Brice, he is not saved."

What?" he said, "He's a pastor."

I said, "I know, but the Lord says he is not saved."

That gave Brice a lot to think about.

We all went back to my sister's home for dinner. After dinner, as my sister Doetha, Brice's wife Bonnie, and I were washing up the dishes, I said, "Could we go to a different church tonight?"

My sister said, "I went to this church that has a traveling choir, and it's a good church."

Bonnie said, "There's one over by us, and they get pretty loud and sing loud too."

Come to find out, they were talking about the same church.

When we were through in the kitchen, we went into the living room and said, "We're going to a different church tonight."

The men said, "We'll go to our regular church tonight, as they're having Putt-Putt golf for the kids afterward.

We ladies and Darla (who was three years old) went to the "noisy" church; and when I walked in the door, I suddenly felt at home. We went in and sat down near the back. The church was full; the music was wonderful. A man was playing the piano and a lady was playing the organ.

A man began talking and said the pastor was away, but the assistant pastor would have the service tonight.

We all sang the Christmas songs. Then, later, after the pastor spoke for a while, he said, "Let's just gather around the altar for a time of prayer."

People began going to the front, but no one in my row moved.

I thought, "I've got to get down there, as I have to find out why I felt at home here." I went down to the altar so I could find out what was going on. I Said, "Lord, how come I feel at home here when this isn't my home?"

He said, "This is gonna be your home."

I said, "How can this be? What about my church back home and what about Barney?"

The Lord said, "I'm the God of impossibilities. I'll work it all out."

As I was thinking about all He had said, I heard a lady crying and sobbing. I looked up, and it was Bonnie, my sister-in-law. I moved over by her and put my arm around her.

Her little daughter was on the platform looking at us. She looked at me and said, "Hey you guys, do you know you are crying?"

I said, "Yes, but it's a happy cry."

When Bonnie was through at the altar, she stood up and said, "Brice will come to this church; I'll see to it."

On the way to church that night, she had said, "I'm going where Brice goes to church." Now, she felt different.

Praise God! The Lord had different plans for them.

As everyone had a few days off after Christmas, we all gathered at my sister's home. We had Bible study, singing, and praying for each other. What a glorious time.

The last evening we were there, my niece and her husband invited me to their home for a time of prayer. After we had prayed for the different ones, I sat in the chair and asked them to pray for me. I said, "Just pray for me, but don't say anything. I just want the Lord to speak to me."

While they were praying, the Lord said, "I have sat you in this place."

I didn't say anything to anyone, but had my answer.

Experience 30. Back to Michigan for a Time

(Chapter 41)

The next morning, it was time for us to leave to go home. Everyone had been blessed, and God was making changes in all of our lives. We put all the luggage in our car and started for Michigan and home.

When we were almost to Georgia, I said, "Would you like to know what the Lord told me while we were here?"

Everyone said, "Yes."

I told them that the Lord said Florida was going to be our home.

The kids got so excited. Kevin said, "Good, let's go back right now."

I told him we have to wait until the Lord says it's time.

We got back home in two days. I told them to not say anything, as it might be years before the Lord says to go.

A few months later, Kevin said to me, "Come and see my room, Mom."

So we walked down the hall to his room. There were boxes stacked up against the wall. He had taken down all of his model cars and things he had on his walls.

I said, "What do you want me to see?"

He said, "I'm all ready to move to Florida: I have my cars all packed."

I said, "But the Lord hasn't told us to move yet."

He replied, "Mom, I just want to be ready."

My kids know that if God told me something, it was gonna happen.

In the meantime, Barney didn't usually come home for supper. We didn't see much of him.

One night, he came home and the kids were in the family room, talking. They were talking about when we live in Florida.

My husband heard them and said to me, "Get out in the living room."

I went out there, and he said, "What's all this talk about going to Florida? I'm not going to Florida!"

I replied, "You don't have to go to Florida. God said I would be living there someday."

He replied angrily, "Well, I'm not going!"

I tried to tell him that the Lord had told me that I would be living in Florida, and it might not be till I'm 90 years old.

"Well, I'm not going!" he said. Then he turned and walked out the door and drove away.

I went back to the family room and told the kids what had happened. They made sure they were alone when they talked about Florida.

Experience 31. The Lord Answers Prayer Again
(Chapter 42)

When Michael, our oldest son, turned 18 years old, he was drafted into the army. I couldn't believe they would take him, as he couldn't see much without his glasses. He got his notice to show up to go to army camp.

He was dating at that time, so they decided to get married.

Two weeks later, he left for army camp.

When his basic training was over, he came home for a few days and then was sent to Fort Sill, Oklahoma. After he was stationed there for a while, he got a leave and came home and took his wife back with him. (He worked as a mechanic on large equipment.)

In the meantime, Terry (our oldest daughter) graduated from high school. She was engaged to Gary at the time, and they were planning their wedding. Terry was thinking that Mike couldn't be at her wedding, so she decided to have her wedding on Mike's birthday, September 17th. We all knew that Michael had no money for him and Darlene (his wife) to fly home. I persuaded Barney that we could pay for Mike and Darlene to fly home. Terry was so surprised when Michael showed up for her big day.

After the wedding and Mike's leave was up, I drove him and his wife back to the airport. Just before they were to board the plane, Mike said, "Mom, I'm on the list to go to Viet Nam."

Thinking about this and his problem seeing without his glasses, I said, "We'll see about that."

He said, "Mom, now don't go writing to the army or the president, because if your name is on the list, you're going!"

I said, "I have a friend I can talk to (meaning Jesus)."

He replied, "There's nothing you can do." Then they boarded the plane and flew back to Oklahoma.

On the way home from the airport in Detroit, I talked to the Lord, "Lord, You know if he should lose his glasses, he might wander over into the enemy territory and get himself killed -- *Help*!"

A couple of weeks later, on my way to church, I was burdened down with worry about Michael. As soon as I got to the church, all the others hurried into their Sunday school classes, and I hurried to my classroom and began to pray about Michael.

The pastor opened the door and asked me what was the matter.

I told him my burden for my son, and he said, "Just keep on praying until you get an answer. I'll have someone teach your class in another room."

I said, "Lord, Michael thinks he's saved and the devil will get him into the fighting and kill him."

The Lord said, "Didn't I save you when you thought you were saved? Don't you think I can do that for him too?"

I said, "Yes Lord, I know You can and You'll take care of him."

Relieved, I went out to the church service to play the organ.

I testified that the Lord was going to take care of Michael, that everything would be all right. *Praise God*!

That afternoon, the phone rang, and the operator asked if I'd accept a collect call from Michael.

I said, "Yes."

Michael was so excited. He said, "Mom, I've been taken off the list. You didn't write to the army or the president, did you?"

I told him I just talked to my special friend Jesus, and He worked it out.

He was relieved, as he didn't want me to try and get special favors for him.

He finished his time in Oklahoma. Another answer to prayer.

Experience 32. Teaching Bible Stories
(Chapter 43)

After a few years of attending the little church I had been saved in, I began to have dreams every night. My dreams were about having a summer "Children's Bible School" for the neighborhood kids.

The Lord showed me the whole program: what songs to sing, the activities for the kids to do, the playtime, etc. The Lord kept telling me to go to the pastor to tell him about it, so I told the pastor about it.

He said, "We've never had anything like that, and I don't think we could do something like that."

I didn't take "No" for an answer. I just kept after him until he said I could do it.

I got busy talking to the church ladies to sell it to them. I got flyers, and we (my kids and I) took them to every door and hung them there. All the information about the Bible school was on the flyer.

The first day, the yard was full of neighborhood kids. We lined them up and marched them into the church, singing a song the Lord said to use. Everything ran smoothly.

For their break-time, we had cookies the ladies had made and Kool-Aid.

The kids were all so excited. We taught them that Jesus loved them, and He could save them.

The pastor was amazed. Each day, it seemed more kids came, and this went on for two weeks.

The last night, we had a program to show their folks what they had learned. Each child was given a Bible. The church was so full of parents and grandparents that some had to sit in the balcony.

One little girl came to me later and said her mom told her, "Why didn't the big church they attended have a Bible school? This is a little church, and they did it."

That was the only year we held Bible school and had over 100 kids attend from the area. The Lord knew just what we needed to do to "Shine His Light" in that neighborhood.

Experience 33. God's Longsuffering Love for my Husband

(Chapter 44)

One Sunday night, about three years after I was saved, my husband said he was going to church with me.

I was so surprised, as he avoided any talk about church. He also acted like he was afraid of me since my great change when I was born again.

When we went into church, everyone greeted us and made him feel more comfortable.

We had a visiting pastor from Detroit that night, and I had never met him before.

The service started off with singing. Folks raised their hands in worship and praise. I did too, as I never bit my fingernails again after the night I was born again. I felt it was an outward sign of an inward work. I wasn't ashamed of my hands anymore.

As the service progressed, one of the older ladies gave a message in Tongues, and there was an interpretation. I had learned about the Holy Spirit and the gifts of the Spirit of Tongues and interpretation over the last couple of years.

My husband looked confused. The message that came was, "There is someone here tonight that I have wooed many times. This is your last chance. If you don't come to me tonight, you will harden your heart and stiffen your neck, and I will never draw you again. This is your last chance. Come to me tonight!"

It was very quiet in the service, and suddenly, the pastor from Detroit also gave a message in Tongues. He also brought the interpretation. It was the identical message, word-for-word, that the first message had been.

I knew immediately that these messages were for my husband. I had remembered in times past, in my previous church when the "Altar Call" was given, my husband would grip the seat in front of him so tightly; his hands would shake. It was quiet after the pastor spoke; no one made a sound.

I kept thinking, "Please get up and go to the altar. The Lord says this is your last chance. Go!"

My husband fidgeted around, but didn't offer to move. I got so upset, I hurried down to the altar to pray for him. He sat right there. I'm sure he knew the Lord meant him.

No one responded to that call from the Lord, and the service resumed. The pastor from Detroit preached, but I wasn't giving him my undivided attention. All I could think of was what the Lord said, "This is your *last chance*, your last chance!"

After the service was ended, we visited with different ones; and we said our good-byes and started driving toward home.

I knew if I said anything, I would start crying, for I was realizing the enormity of it all.

Finally, after we had driven along in silence for a while, I said, "Do you know who the Lord was talking to tonight?"

He replied, "Oh, that guy that was sitting in front of us and crying."

I said, "No, he is already saved. The Lord was talking to someone else who isn't saved. Don't you know who the Lord was talking to?"

It was very quiet for a few minutes, and then he said, "Ya, me."

I asked in disbelief, "You mean, you knew it was the Lord that was talking to you, and you didn't respond?"

He looked over at me and said angrily, "Listen here, I don't want to get saved. Now leave me alone!"

Shocked, I didn't say anything more, as I realized that tonight was really his last chance. I never mentioned it to him again, but I kept on praying, "Lord, give him another chance."

Experience 34. Barney Gets Another Chance

(Chapter 45)

Quite some time had passed; it was almost a year when Barney said he wanted to go to church with me.

I was so happy, for I thought that, maybe the Lord was going to give him another chance.

As we were walking into the church, he seemed to be very happy. He was talking to me, which was very unusual, for he very seldom ever spoke to me.

As the service moved on and the Altar Call was given, he jumped up from his seat and hurried toward the altar.

The pastor looked up and said, "Barney, do you want to get saved?"

Barney replied, "Yes."

The pastor said to kneel down. He then asked several of the men to come and pray with him. They knelt down, and just a few minutes, Barney stood up.

The pastor looked at him and asked, "Well, Barney, are you saved?"

Barney said he was.

The pastor said, "Well, tell us about it."

Barney began to ramble on about how God wants us to be missionaries and go all over the world.

When I listened to what he said, it was just a bunch of words he had heard others say. I knew he wasn't saved. I was so disappointed.

My Baptist friend Mary had told Barney before that, when he got saved, she wanted him to call and tell her.

When we got home, I went to the phone and dialed Mary's number and handed Barney the phone and said, "You know you told Mary you'd call her when you got saved."

When Mary answered the phone, he said, "They finally got me."

I wanted to believe he was saved, but the next morning, he was more miserable acting than usual.

Later that morning, I drove over to Betty's and told her, "He is not saved; I wish he was, but he is not."

About that time, the phone rang, and it was the pastor. Betty told him I was there, and he wanted to talk to me.

"Well, is he saved?"

"No, he isn't," I replied.

"Sister, do you doubt God?" he asked.

"No, I don't doubt God; I doubt man," I answered. "I am sorry, but he is not saved,"

"Well," he said, "let's just wait and see."

Weeks went by, and the pastor paid a call on Barney at his business. Barney was busy working.

The pastor confronted Barney, but Barney just kept avoiding him. Finally, the pastor walked up to him and pinned him up against the wall and asked him, "Barney, I just want to ask you one question: Are you saved? Just tell me, 'yes' or 'no!' Are you saved?"

Barney replied, "Well, if you mean saved like you and Donna, 'No,' I'm not!"

The pastor said, "Okay, just one more question: Do you want to be saved?"

Barney replied, "No."

The pastor backed away from him in shock and said, "All right, then your blood will not be on my hands. I won't bother you anymore."

After this, the pastor left. He never told me about this visit, but my son Bill was working there and had seen-and-heard the whole thing.

I continued to pray, "Lord, give him another chance."

One day, the Lord just said to me, "Stop praying for me to give him another chance. He has had his last chance. You know I mean what I say."

So that settled that. It made me very sad, but he had made his own choice. God doesn't send people to hell: They make their own choice, I'm sorry to say.

Experience 35. Donna's Vision
(Chapter 46)

One afternoon, I was kneeling at a chair praying in the living room. I had been in prayer for some time. I had a most unusual experience. I was awake; and with my eyes closed, I had a vision:

All of a sudden, I saw my husband lying dead in a casket in a local funeral home. It was as if I was above the scene watching what was going on. I could see people coming in this funeral home and walking over to me and talking to me. I couldn't see their faces, but I knew they were friends. Then I saw two of my lady-friends standing there and talking to me. It was 9:00 p.m. And the attendant, who had been by the door, had walked away. Then I saw my son Bill standing there. A man came late, and he said to Bill that he was his mom's friend. Bill walked him over to me, and the man said, "Sister,

I came as soon as I heard. I was at a prayer-meeting in a different town when someone told me your husband died."

Then the vision ended.

I wondered what all that was about. I hadn't been praying for my husband, as the Lord had told me not to.

I didn't tell anyone about the vision, but sometimes I would ponder it over in my mind. My husband began spending less time at home.

On Sunday mornings, the kids would ask him to go to church with us. He didn't work on Sunday mornings, but he would just give them different excuses why he couldn't go. Finally, he started getting up earlier and would leave before the kids would say anything to him. I told the kids to just leave him alone. He is not interested in church.

Experience 36. Donna's Release
(Chapter 47)

My husband got very secretive. He would never tell us what he was doing or where he had been spending his time. He never told me anything, even when I asked him. He would just shrug his shoulders and walk away.

He closed his meat business and got another job. We didn't know where he was working.

After a few months, the kids found out where he was working and told me. It was in the meat department of a small grocery store.

Barny told me, one day, that the money he made was his money; and if I wanted any money, I should go to work.

I asked him, "What about the kids? What about food and clothes for the kids?"

He just said, "That is your problem."

I got to the point that I prayed for every quart of milk and every loaf of bread. God was teaching me to live by faith and to rely completely on Him. It seemed, whenever I needed money to pay a bill or for food, someone would call me and want me to clean an apartment for them or do some painting or wash walls. I would earn enough to take care of that bill or need. The Lord had told me He didn't want me to have a regular job; He would provide. *Praise God*!

The first part of September 1970, our preacher had left, and an evangelist was to be at our church for a week of meetings. As he preached, his wife sat up on the platform behind him.

I was sitting close to the front, as I was the organist.

He looked over to me and he said, "Sister, would you close in prayer?"

I prayed and then began to cry. No one noticed, as everyone was moving around talking to each other.

I said, "Lord, why am I crying? What is going on?" I looked up and saw the evangelist's wife coming toward me. I held out my hand to her, as I thought she was coming to say good-bye.

She took my hand in both of hers and said, "Sister! The Lord tells me you are carrying a mighty heavy burden."

I said, "Oh, with God's help I manage."

She said, "Well, Sister, He says to just thank Him and praise Him, because He is going to lift that burden very, very soon!"

When she said that, something in me said, "He is going to die."

As I drove home from church that night and as I dropped off the folks that had ridden with me, I was deep in thought about what that lady had told me.

When I got home, there was no one there. I knelt down at a chair and began to pray. I said, "Lord, I can't thank You and praise You, knowing that he is going to die a year sooner, or a month sooner, or a day sooner. I know he is not going to Heaven, as he has rejected You and chose the other. Eternity is forever, and I don't want anyone to go to hell."

My heart was very heavy that night, knowing what was going to happen.

The next morning was Labor Day. I sat at the breakfast table with my husband, not knowing if he was going to work, or what. I asked him if he heard that our son Mike (who was out of the army now) might be getting a job as a mechanic on the school buses.

He just shrugged his shoulders and got up and walked out the door and got in his truck and drove away.

I thought, "If only you knew what the Lord told me last night."

Well, he didn't come home that evening. But he didn't come home regularly anyhow, so I wasn't surprised.

Melanie and Kevin were in the family room watching TV. I was in the kitchen.

Around 9:00 p.m., the phone rang, and it was the lady at the store where our son Denny worked pumping gas. When I answered, she said, "Mrs. Bonkoski, I don't want to be telling tales out of school, but did you know your husband has been taken to the hospital?"

I said, "No."

She said, "Mr. LaRue called here and told Dennis to come to the hospital about his dad."

I told her I'd go to the hospital right away, and I thanked her for calling me.

When I hung up the phone, I went out and told Kevin and Melanie what Mrs. Wedge called for.

They just said, "Okay."

The Lord said to me, "You are not going anyplace. He doesn't want you there. This is what I told you was going to happen."

I thought, "That means there is going to be a funeral and company."

Just then, the phone rang again. It was Dennis. He said, "Mom, Dad just had a heart attack and died."

I told him I would come to the hospital. When I got there, a nurse was waiting for me with papers to sign. One was for an autopsy.

I said, "Why?"

She said, "Because he wasn't under a doctor's care."

So I signed the papers, and she handed me his boots and a bag with his billfold. There was nothing in the billfold except his driver's license and the kids' school pictures.

The nurse asked me what funeral home to call, and I told her. (It was the one in my vision.)

Experience 37. My Husband Passes On
(Chapter 48 & 49)

My husband had passed away, and I had to go to the funeral home and make the arrangements. My friend Betty called me and said she would drive me there.

As I waited for her, I thought to myself, "I only have $5.00, so how am I going to pay for a funeral and all that it entails?"

My son spoke up and said, "Mom, we know that Dad must have hidden money over in the old meat-shop. Can we go over there and look?" (We still owned the meat-shop and the house and the property.)

I thought for a minute and then said, "If you want to go and look, it is fine with me, but I don't think you will find anything."

Betty came and drove me to the funeral home. When we arrived, she said, "I'll just wait in the car."

As I walked inside, I thought, "Lord, help me. I have never done anything like this before, so You are going to have to help me."

I made the arrangements and I walked back out to Betty's car. I told Betty that it was all taken care of. I said, "It really doesn't matter how much it is going to cost: I only have $5.00, so the Lord will have to take care of it."

When I arrived home, I went inside. My children were there and standing around the kitchen table waiting for me. In the center of the table were little packages of money. Each one was wrapped in waxed paper. Mike and the others found these packages of money stuck between the cement blocks in the walls of the meat-shop. Some of the packages were found tucked under drawers and in other places.

I said, "Open them up and let's see what he was hiding!"

After all the excitement of finding so much money, they began to count it. There was a total of $1,500.00. We were so surprised. None of us had ever seen that much money before. I had not had any money for a long time to buy new clothes or shoes for the kids. I thought, "The kids are going to have new shoes and new clothes for the funeral."

I gave each of the kids money for new clothes and shoes, and they went shopping. I also had money to pay the household bills. *"Thank you, Lord!"*

We didn't have a regular pastor at our church at the time, so I asked a pastor-friend from a nearby town to handle the funeral service.

On the last night of the viewing, a man (I previously had received a vision of) came running in and said, "Sister, I came as soon as I heard. I was at a prayer-meeting in a different town when someone told me your husband died." This was exactly, word-for-word, just as my vision had shown me. Then I knew it was all in God's plan. (See Experience 35 [Chapter 46].)

There were a lot of people at the funeral, as my husband had many friends that he had been supplying meat for many years. So, many were surprised that he died so young, as he was only 45 years old. I found out later that heart-trouble ran in his family: His father had fallen over dead on the street in a nearby city at the age of 54; his brother died of a heart attack at a dance a few years later. This was a shock to our family, as my husband had never had physical problems.

After I had the vision of his death, I would ask the Lord occasionally how He was going to take care of the funeral bill.

One day, I happened to think if there was any money left in the bank account for his business. His checkbook was gone, so I thought, "I think I will call the bank." I made the call and told the lady at the bank that my husband had died, and he had an account there; and I wondered if there was any money left in the account.

She asked me if my name was on the account.

I said, "Yes."

She said she would check.

I remembered how my husband had put my name on the account so I could help him write checks for the business and take care of some of the bookkeeping for him.

The lady came back to the phone and said, "There is $7,000.00 left in the account."

I said, "Lord, he is going to pay for his own funeral."

The coroner Dr. Kopp called to tell me the results of the autopsy. He said Barney's heart had just literally burst. There was no way he could have lived.

It was so sad. This experience happened about five years after my born-again experience, and it was eight years since the accusations had started in 1962.

Experience 38. Time for a Move
(Chapter 50)

Life went on day by day. I asked the Lord what He wanted me to do. He had taken care of the funeral expenses, so that wasn't a problem. I kept going to our little church and the ladies' prayer meetings every week in our homes. I waited on the Lord for directions. Some of my friends suggested that I find a different husband, but I wasn't interested in a husband; I just waited to hear from the Lord.

Two months later, the Lord spoke to me. He said, "Now it is time to move to Florida."

It was nearly Thanksgiving Day. We always had Thanksgiving dinner at our home. All of my six children gathered together with their families, and we had a wonderful dinner.

After everything was cleared away, we just sat and talked. I told them that the Lord spoke to me and said, "Now it is time to move to Florida." I then said, "We will probably go the first part of December."

The next day, my son Bill called and said he and his wife and her two children were going to move with us too. In just a short time, Michael called and said he and his family wanted to move with us also.

Then my daughter Terry and her family said they weren't moving: They would stay, as they both had good jobs and a little girl.

My daughter Melanie baby-sat for the couple across the road, so I asked her to go ask Kent to come over. He was in real estate, and maybe he would like to list our home for sale. He was happy to list our home, and the third couple that looked at it bought it immediately.

I had sister Doetha living in Orlando, plus brother Brice. After the Lord told me to sell the house and move to Florida, I called my sister and told her I would send her money if she could rent us three houses there.

She found three homes, so we could unload the moving van when we arrived.

The van had gone to my oldest son Mike's place first and loaded up this furniture. Then they came to my place and took all of our things. My other son lived some distance away, so we followed the moving van to his place in Pontiac and waited while they picked up his household things. As the moving van left, we followed it in our four vehicles.

It began to snow, and by the time we got to Bowling Green, Ohio, we couldn't see the moving van anymore. It was snowing so hard, we couldn't hardly see. So we stopped at a motel to rest and started again the next morning.

We had our own little caravan. We got to Orlando that night. We stayed with our relatives there.

In the morning, the moving van arrived and unloaded our things in the three homes my sister had rented for us. We were so happy to be out of the snow and cold weather.

We were only there for a few weeks when I drove over to my niece's house. Just before I got there, the Lord said, "If you will look to your right, you will see your new home."

It was just across the street from my niece's home. I looked to the right and saw a nice home. I said, "Lord, I wasn't looking for another house; I like the one I am living in now."

He said, "That is your new home."

I stopped the car immediately and noticed a small home-made sign about 1-foot-high in the front yard: "For Sale." I backed the car up to the corner and turned right. The house was on the corner, so I just drove around to the carport.

I walked up and knocked at the door of the sunporch. The lady inside came to greet me. I told her I wanted to look at the house.

She said, "Oh, it is a mess, as we are packing to move back to Fort Myers. We've just been here so our daughter could go to the Seventh Day Adventist school just down-and-across the street."

I told her that didn't matter, but the house must have three bedrooms and hardwood floors.

She said, "It has three bedrooms and hardwood floors."

I went in and walked through the house, and it was lovely. I looked at her and said, "I'll take it. Would you prefer check or do you prefer cash?"

She looked shocked and said, "You can't buy it just like that!"

I said, "Well, you have it for sale, don't you?"

The lady replied, "But there is another lady that wants to buy it, and I am to hear from her in three days."

I told her, "The Lord told me this was my new home, so I will be back in three days to close the deal."

She watched me leave rather stunned-looking.

Three days later, I told my two youngest kids to come with me to see our new home. When we got there, the lady said, "Well, I guess you were right, as the other lady never called." She looked at me like she was trying to figure me out: She asked, "Are you a missionary?"

I laughed and said, "No, I am just a 'Jesus People'."

I didn't know that God would tell me which house to buy, but we were all moved-in within just a few days. God is concerned about everything we do and even where we live. *Praise the Lord*!

Experience 39. The Carburetor Adventure

(Chapter 51)

In everything give thanks, for this is the will of the Lord. . ..

Early one spring evening, the phone rang; and as I answered, my sister's voice asked, "What are you and Kevin going to do tonight?"

"Well, we hadn't planned anything in particular," I said, "what did you have in mind?"

She said, "We'd like you to come over and spend the evening with us and maybe play a few games of Aggravation or something else. How does that sound to you?"

I turned to Kevin and told him what she had said, and he smiled and said he'd really like that. He enjoyed being with his aunt and uncle. I turned back to the phone and told her that we would be over soon.

We always had lots of fun and plenty of laughs as we tried to outwit each other. We would play partners, and the fellows would win a turn and it would make us all the more determined to win the next time. Such a happy time of sharing in just good, clean fun.

After we played games, my brother-in-law would grin and say, "Well, time for a coffee break."

This always meant we would all go to the kitchen and have coffee-or-milk and some goodies, such as cookies or cake or something sweet.

Later, happy-and-tired and too full, I stood up and said it was time that we started home. We said our good-byes and went outside into the warm Florida evening. The moon was shining down on us, and we could smell the fragrances of the flowers in the area.

As we started to drive away, my sister and her husband turned and walked back into their home. I had only driven down the street about 20 feet when the car slowed down and stalled. I pulled the car over to the curb and tried to start it. Over-and-over I kept turning the key, but it wouldn't start. This was a brand-new car I was driving, as I had turned in my old car for a new one.

I looked over at Kevin, and as our eyes met, we both began to laugh. He said, "I guess we had better push the car back in front of Aunt Doetha's house."

We climbed out and ran around to the front of the car and began to push it backwards. Kevin smiled and said, "At least there isn't any snow here, and it's warm; huh, Mom?"

We were both laughing as we went back to their door and rang the bell.

When they opened it, they were so surprised to see us again so soon.

"Would you give us a ride home, Aunt Doetha, as our car quit on us and we need a ride?" Kevin was laughing all the time he was talking.

She looked at him in disbelief, and I said, "We really do need a ride home. The car did quit, but I will come over and pray for it in the morning and then take it home." (Why I didn't pray for it then, I don't know.)

She turned and got her car keys and followed us out the door. I guess she didn't know if we were trying to pull a joke on her or not.

We all got into her car and she backed out into the street. I am not sure if we were really going through with it or not. After we had gone a few blocks, she could see that we really were serious and that the car really wouldn't run.

As she pulled up in front of our home, she said, "Oh, there is Brice over across the street at Evelyn's house." (Brice was my brother and Evelyn was my niece.) Kevin and Doetha got out of the car and started to walk across the street to Evelyn's house.

I said, "Hey, where are you guys going?"

"Well, we are going to go and tell Brice that your car won't run, and he will go over and get it going and bring it home," they said as they kept on walking away from me.

"You don't have to do that. I'll go over and pray for it in the morning and bring it home myself," I hollered after them.

They kept right on walking in the opposite direction. I turned around and walked into my house; and in a few minutes, the two of them returned with Brice and Tom, Evelyn's husband.

Brice walked over to me and held out his hand and said, "Let me take your keys, and we'll go over and get your car running. If we can't' get it to run, we'll tow it home for you."

"You don't have to do that; I'll go over in the morning and pray for it and bring it home myself."

He just stood there looking at me and holding out his hand for the keys. I could see that what I was saying wasn't changing his plans, so I handed him the keys, and the three fellows turned and started to leave.

"It won't run, so bring it home if you want to, but I'll get it going tomorrow," I kept telling them.

I could see that I wasn't the only one in the family with determinations. I turned to my sister and said, "You know, I don't know why I just didn't pray for the car tonight."

She just looked at me like she didn't know what was going on.

In about 20 minutes, we looked out the window and there was all three of them towing my car up the street behind their car. They came back to the house and looked sort of perplexed.

Brice said, "I don't know just what is the matter with it, but I'll stop by on my way home from work and will bring my tools and get it running for you tomorrow."

I could see that it was futile to try to change his mind.

The next morning, Kevin hopped on his bike and rode off to school.

I looked outside, and it was a beautiful day. The sun was shining and everything was quite peaceful out. I thought to myself, "Now is the time to go out and start the car."

I climbed in under the steering wheel and tried the switch. I wanted to be sure that it was still not running. It acted the same as it had the night before.

I got back out of the car and walked around to the front of the hood. I sensed in my spirit, after praying about it, that the problem was in the carburetor. I reached under and unhooked the hood-latch and lifted the hood up. I reached over and loosened the screw from the air filter pan. Lifting it off, I could see the carburetor. I leaned over the side and reached in and laid my hand on the carburetor and said, "In the name of Jesus, I command you to run!" I lifted my hand off and replaced the air filter pan. I adjusted the screw and walked around and closed the hood. Then I turned, climbed back into the car and turned on the ignition. Vroom. . .. The engine started immediately. *Praise the Lord*! There hadn't been any doubt in my mind that it wouldn't start.

Later that afternoon, Brice drove in behind my car that was still sitting in the carport. He began to get out of his car, and reaching behind his seat, he started to lift out his tool box.

I ran out the door and told him to leave his tools in the car. He turned around and looked at me with a questioning look on his face. "Why?" he said.

"Well, I just prayed for it this morning, and it runs fine," I said. I told him that I felt it was the carburetor, and so I just prayed for that part.

I couldn't tell if he believed me or not, but I thought to myself, "It is so great to have the Holy Spirit in me to tell me these things so I can know what to do when a problem arises." *Praise the Lord*!

He got into my car and turned the key, and it started immediately. He turned around and looked at me and just smiled.

Experience 40. A Janitor Again

(Chapter 52)

One morning, my brother stopped by and said they were having a problem with the janitor at their church. He has some personal problems, and they needed someone to help him until he was better.

Brice said, "Because you used to be the janitor at your old church, I am asking you if you would help him."

"The Lord told me that I am not to take a job," I said.

"You don't have to take the job; just come and help him for a few weeks until he is better," he said.

I prayed about it, and the Lord said I could help him for a short time. I called my brother, and he said to be at the church on Monday morning to meet the janitor.

I went there and met the janitor, and he told me where to clean. Before I started cleaning, I had to meet the pastor.

The pastor asked me into his office and asked me why I wanted to work at their church.

I told him my brother had asked me to come and help the janitor until he felt better.

After questioning me for 20 minutes, he let me leave so I could get to work. I couldn't understand why all of the questions were necessary: I was only going to dust, scrub floors, and vacuum-and-clean.

I worked there for 2 weeks, and on the third week, I was mopping the cement floor between the pews when the Lord said, "These people are a stench in my nostrils and an abomination in my sight."

I said, "Whoa, Lord, I don't go to this church, and I don't want to know anything about these people."

The Lord didn't stop. He kept on speaking line-after-line. He said that people came here carrying their problems and left with the same problems-and-burdens they came in with. They come in sick and leave sick. Back-sliders could sit at ease in this church. God said, "They are not following me in this church, but men are running it."

There was a lot more to the message that God gave me, and I was shocked at what He said. When He was through, He said, "Now go tell the pastor."

Oh no, I wasn't going to tell the pastor! Every time I would see him, he would say things like, "Praise the Lord, Sister" and "God

Bless you, Sister." I knew he wasn't going to accept any message from me.

Experience 41. A Hard Word to Deliver
(Chapter 53)

When I finished my work, I left in a hurry.

After dinner that night, the Lord said, "Because you wouldn't tell the pastor the message I gave you, now you can write it down on paper and send it to him."

I got paper and pen; and as fast as I could write, the Lord was telling me every word and Scripture to write. When He finished telling me what to write, I had two full sheets of typing-paper filled. He told me to put it in an envelope with the pastor's name on it and mail it. He also said to sign my name on it. That was Tuesday night, and the pastor received it the next day.

On Wednesday, after church, I came home. I had told my sister and showed her the copy of the letter I had made.

She didn't say anything except, "We'll wait and see."

When Brice stopped by after church, he asked me how my service was, and I told him it was okay.

When I asked him how his church service was, he said, "Someone wrote the pastor a letter, and he was really mad. I would like to know what was in that letter."

I walked over to my bill-caddy, took out the letter and handed it to him.

He looked at me very shocked and asked, "You didn't write that letter, did you?"

I answered, "Yes, I wrote it, but I only wrote what the Lord told me to write. This was from God to the pastor and the church. I'd never write it unless He told me to write it: I would be afraid of what God might do to me."

Well, the next week, when I walked by his office to clean, it was all quiet. In all the offices, there wasn't a sound.

I cleaned the Sanctuary and the Nursery, and when I came out carrying the vacuum, the pastor was waiting for me.

I began to walk past him, and he said, "Just a minute, Donna." (I was thinking, "Where is all this, 'Praise the Lord,' and 'God Bless you,' etc.)

I stopped, noticing how quiet it was, for no typewriters were going or no talking was going on as usual. I knew everyone was listening.

I said, "Yes."

155

The pastor said, "You are a False Prophetess!"

I said, "No, I am not!"

He said, "Oh yes, you are. You wrote that letter and you are a False Prophetess!"

I replied, "No, I'm not; I am not stupid enough to write down something and say it is from God; God could strike me dead. God told me to give this message before and I didn't do it, so He told me to write it."

The pastor said, "You are a False Prophetess!" (He spoke it out very loudly.)

I said, "Listen, if you don't think that is from God, why don't you tear it up and throw it away?"

Then he said, "I and the board-members are going to discuss this letter, and then we want you to come to a meeting with us."

I replied, "Name the time and the place, and I will be there."

He handed me an envelope and I left.

I went to a different building and gave the check in it to the janitor. (He always paid me.) I let him read the letter the pastor wrote about me being a False Prophetess.

The janitor had a few things to say about what was going on there too.

Well, I guess you know I was never asked to meet with the board or anyone. I never heard another word about it. I left there in a few weeks, as the janitor was better. *

_____

* *Note*: Ten years later, after going many places for the lord, I came back to Orlando for a short time. People would say to me, "You must have been wrong about that message to the pastor and to that church."

I knew the Lord had given me that message, so I would just say, "Wait and see."

Brice's daughter came home from church there one night, and she said, "The pastor gave his resignation tonight, and the board accepted it." (The pastor didn't think they would.)

Things have been going on for years, and he didn't think anyone knew about it. Someone was going to expose him. I guess he thought he had the people fooled, but God sees everything.

I heard before this that the Head of the Music Department left his wife-and-children and ran off with another man [sic] from here. That man called himself a "pastor," but he made the front page of the local newspaper in disgrace. He was asked to leave the denomination that he was in.

I didn't care what that man called me: I knew God never lies! *He is Faithful*!

Experience 42. Working at Disney World
(Chapter 54)

One day in December, Melanie was talking about going out to Disney World and get a job. Disney World had opened in October, and this was December. She said, "Mom, let's go out to Disney and get a job. We could ride together, and that would be so much fun."

I told her that the Lord had told me that I was not supposed to work a steady job. He said He would take care of us.

She said, "Oh, come on, Mom."

I told her that I would go with her and apply, and if the Lord wanted me to work there, they would hire me; but if He didn't, they wouldn't hire me.

On one of those beautiful sunny days, we drove out to the Disney employment offices. We both filled out an application. Melanie was directed to go for an interview at the "Mickey Mouse" building.

When we returned to the main building, Melanie asked me if I was hired.

I told her that I was to start work as soon as I went to a certain shoe-store in Orlando. I was to pick up a pair of shoes to go with the costume I would be wearing. I would be working on "Main Street."

Excitedly, Melanie said she was hired also. She would be working in the "Contemporary Hotel."

We would be working different shifts, so we had to get Melanie a car to drive back-and-forth to work. It was quite a distance from our home in Orlando. We were excited to be working at the Walt Disney World.

I picked up the shoes I would be wearing and went for my first day. I would be working in the "Emporium." That was a big store on Main Street.

There was a lot of us training, mostly young people in their teens. Then we were taken on a tour. We were shown where we would go when we arrived the next day.

There was a huge parking area for the workers a distance from the park. We would ride from the parking lot to our entrance on buses or trams.

We were shown where to go to pick up our costumes and also see the dressing rooms.

There was a huge cafeteria.

I saw a very large room with people sitting at sewing machines. They were working on costumes.

When we came in from the outside, we would be in long tunnels. There were lights all along the walls. There were elevators which we would ride in to go up to our work areas. Some of us just walked to the elevators, while others rode in trams. They went to far-areas to work, and this was all underground.

Melanie and I wouldn't be working together; we wouldn't even be working the same hours. I would work days, and Melanie would work afternoons.

I worked on Main Street, wearing an 1890's costume with the floor-length skirt.

Melanie would work in the Contemporary Hotel. She worked on the floor that the monorail went through. When the monorail went through there, you could look down and see Melanie working.

We got Melanie a nice car, and we both began driving to Disney World to start our new jobs.

I wasn't out there to just work, but that the Lord had a reason for my job. I asked the Lord, "Do you want me to talk to someone that works her or am I here to pray for someone?"

I heard no response.

People came there from all over the world, and some I couldn't talk to, because they spoke a different language.

One day, a lady came and said, "I'm lost."

When I looked at her, it was a friend from our ladies' prayer meeting back home in Michigan. It was so good to see her, but she really was lost. I took her over to the train station to the "Lost and Found." She found her family was there looking for her.

Another day, a man came into the "Emporium," and he was holding a camera. He walked over to my area, and he asked me to go outside so he could take a picture of me.

I said, "Go outside and take a picture of one of the cute girl guides."

He said, "No, I want your picture."

Finally, he left with no pictures.

Hours later, the cameraman was back; only this time, he had his wife with him. He said to her, "This is the lady I want to take a picture of."

I said, "Why?"

He said, "Because where I work, we make your skirts, and I wanted a picture of a lady wearing one of our skirts."

Experience 43. What is Stuck in my Drain?

(Chapter 55)

The sun was shining in through the windows, and it was a glorious Florida morning. The birds outside were twittering and flying from tree-to-tree, and we were scurrying around inside our home.

Kevin was rushing around gathering his things to take to school, and I was standing in the kitchen, looking at the sink. It was stopped-up again. I had just borrowed my niece's plunger and returned it the day before. (She just lived across the street.)

I thought, "No, I'm not going to borrow it again." I proceeded to fill both sides of the double sink full of very hot water. Kevin was ready for me to drive him to school, so I just left the hot water in the sink, hoping that it would take care of whatever was stopping-up the drain.

I drove him to school and hurried back home, as I had to get ready for work at Disney World. When I entered the house, I went straight to the kitchen. The water hadn't gone down even a fraction of an inch. I just stood there looking at it and wondering what I was going to do.

"Hey," I said, "I'm a child of the living God, and I don't have to put up with this. I have all authority in the name of Jesus!" I pointed to the sink and said with authority, "In the name of Jesus, I command you to go down!"

It was just like someone had pulled the plug and the water went swirling down with a loud *swooshing* sound, and the sinks were empty.

I stood there in amazement and said, "How come there is never anyone else around to see it when God does these things?"

I hurried and scrubbed out the sinks and then got ready and went to work, but my mind wasn't on what I had to do at work. It was going over the events of that morning. I guess God was teaching me that I could call on Him for everything, not just for the big problems.

Experience 44. The End of My Time at Disney World

(Chapter 56)

A few days later, I clocked out as my shift was over. I went out and was standing in the pick-up area. I would wait there for a bus or tram to take me to my car in the big parking lot.

A lady was standing there waiting. She kept looking at me, and finally she said, "Aren't you the lady that spoke at our church a while back?"

I said, "Yes."

She said she had to leave the service early, but that she had wanted to talk to me.

Instantly, I knew this was the reason I had to be at Walt Disney World: God had it all planned.

"My husband is acting very strange, just like your husband was," she said.

She went on telling me a similar story to mine. She said her husband was in the military, stationed nearby.

He kept a gun under his pillow at night. He said he was going to kill their 2 little boys and make it look like she did it. He had threatened her with this statement. She was terrified for the children and for herself.

I gave her my phone number and told her to call me anytime.

She began to call me, and when we were at work, we would talk. She worked in a shop on Main Street. Sometimes I would skip lunch and go to see her, and she would tell me more of what was going on at her home.

After about two months, God took over the situation. Her husband was acting very strange at his work. The military stepped in and put him in a place to deal with his mental problem.

She called me and said, "God has taken care of my problems." *Praise the Lord.*

I knew my work at Disney was finished. The Lord told me that Thursday was my last day. When I got a chance, I went to my boss. I told him I had to leave.

He said, "Can't you please stay through Sunday?" (It would be Easter, and they would be expecting larger crowds on Easter.)

I asked the Lord, and He said, "No, Thursday is your last day."

I went back to my boss and told him Thursday was my last day: My Boss said so.

Then the boss said, "Who is your boss?"

I said, "God."

He looked surprised; then said, "Okay, go sign the papers."

I only spent three months at Disney.

Experience 45. Searching for the Right Church

(Chapter 57)

I began going to the different Pentecostal Churches to see where I would fit in. Every church I would go to, I would wait for the Lord to tell me "this is the one."

Instead of that, He would say, "Don't put any roots down here."

Finally, after quite a few weeks of that, I finally said, "Lord, I don't know where you want me. I am not leaving here to go to church tonight unless you have someone call me on the phone or come and knock at the door and invite me to a church. Otherwise, I am staying home, for I don't know where to go."

Some hours went by, and I thought, "Well, it looks like I am staying home tonight."

Just then, the phone rang, and it was my sister. She attended a Methodist Church, and I had gone there with her and I told her, "This church is dead. Don't ask me to come here."

She said, "I know you don't like my church, but would you come to my church tonight?"

I said, "Oh no, I don't want to go to your church."

She said, "Well, that is all right. I just thought I would ask you."

Then, I told her what I had told the Lord. I said I didn't want to go there, but I had to, because that must be where the Lord wants me.

I went there that night, but I was hoping the Lord had made a mistake, but He hadn't.

I was very verbal about my salvation and all the things that God was doing in my life and what He had already done. On Wednesday night Bible Study, I would ask the pastor if I could give a testimony, and he would say, "Okay."

They didn't do that at my sister's church, and most of the folks were not very happy with my spouting off, but I was blessed and bubbling over with the love of God and His great blessings. The pastor seemed to enjoy it anyhow.

Every time I would walk into the church, I could see some of them were hoping I wasn't there. I was there every time the church door was open. I would say to the Lord, "Why do you have me here, Lord. They don't want me here, and I don't want to be here either." I never got an answer.

Then, every Saturday afternoon, the pastor began to come by my home and say, "Tell me some more of your stories, testimonies."

I would tell him my experiences for a few hours, and then he would say, "My, you have so much faith."

I would tell him he had as much as me. The Bible says that God gives us a measure of faith. He doesn't give me a big scoop and you a small scoop. He gives us all the same, but we have to exercise our faith like our arm. (Then I would flex my arm and show him what I meant.)

He would continue to say that I had so much faith.

He came for several Saturday afternoons, asking me to tell him more of my stories. Finally, one Saturday, just as he was leaving, he said, "I came today to ask you to join our church."

I was surprised, and I told him, "I don't think the Lord wants me to join your church. The people there don't want me there, and I don't really want to be there."

He just ignored me and said, "If you decide to join tomorrow, just walk down to the front at the last song. Just pray about it."

He left happy and smiling, and I thought, "I am not going to join that church. I am sure the Lord doesn't want me to join, so I'm not even going to pray about it."

The next day, I got ready for church, and I stopped by my sister's to give them a ride to church. I opened their door and asked if they were ready, and they said, "In just a few minutes."

I said, "Hey, do you want to hear something funny? Pastor Vaughn was over yesterday afternoon and asked me to join the church. Did you ever hear anything so funny?"

My brother-in-law said, "I don't think that is funny."

I said, "Well, I'm not going to join that church. I am sure the Lord doesn't want me to join."

When they were ready, we went on to the church. Nothing more was said about it. We went to Sunday school and then the church service, and when it came to the last song, I picked up the song book thinking, "I'm not going to join, so I might just as well sing."

Then, the Lord said very firmly, "Get down there."

I was so shocked. I put the song book down and began to push past my brother-in-law, and he kind of chuckled and said, "Where are you going, Donna?"

I said, "Oh, shut up." I walked down to where the pastor was standing with his head bowed and his eyes closed.

When he looked up, he said, "Donna, I am surprised!"

I said, "Well, what do you think I am?"

So I joined the church. I usually think I know what the Lord wants, but I'm always wrong.

Experience 46. A Full Gospel Businessmen's Meeting
(Chapter 58)

I attended home-prayer meetings, and once a month, I'd attend the Full Gospel Businessmen's Meetings. The meetings were open to everyone.

They had singing and always had a speaker. This man would encourage the others to share their own experiences. They would explain how God had done something wonderful in their life or helped someone else. It was always so great to hear the great testimonies. I even became the piano player for their meetings.

It was announced in one of their meetings that there was going to be a Full Gospel Businessmen's Convention to be held in Tampa, Florida. I knew I wanted to attend that convention. There would be three meetings of testimonies all day. My brother and sister said they wanted to go too, so we made our plans.

Before the convention, I attended a different meeting to hear Derick Prince preach, telling how the Lord was using him in a mighty way. As I was leaving his meeting, I went by his book-table and purchased a little book called, *Expelling Demons*.

The night before we were to go to Tampa to the convention, the Lord kept waking me up. He would say, "Read that little book." The Lord woke me several times, and I would read that little book again.

As I drove to Tampa, I told the others about the Lord waking me to read this book. Two other people went with us, so there were five in my car. We all went to the breakfast-meeting and the afternoon-meeting. We left for a short time to eat supper and returned. At the end of the evening-meeting, I was just sitting with my brother: We were waiting for the others in our group to leave.

A lady came on my left side and began tugging on my sleeve and pointing behind me. She said, "My sister, my sister."

I could see a lady sprawled back on a chair. She reminded me of the lady that had died in a meeting in Detroit, and Brother Bogel had prayed for her and she came back to life.

My brother Brice was sitting by me, and I jumped up and said, "Come on." I ran over to the lady in the chair. She wasn't breathing, so I grabbed ahold of her head and began to pray for her. I didn't pray in English, but I prayed in Tongues.

About that time, another lady came and stood behind the lady in the chair. She kept looking at me and saying, "Leave her alone; she doesn't want you to pray for her."

I kept on praying, and the other woman kept on telling me to stop.

Finally, the lady (in the chair that I was praying for) began to move. She began to wave her hands in the air like she was hitting at something.

The lady behind the chair kept saying, "See, I told you she didn't want you to pray for her."

I thought, "What is going on?"

The woman in the chair was batting the air so much she threw herself off the chair and onto the floor. She never stopped batting the air and saying, "Get away from me; don't touch me." She wasn't looking at me; she was seeing something in the air trying to get to her.

I got down beside her and continued praying for her.

The other woman got down on the other side of her. She put her face close to mine and hissed, "Leave her alone; she doesn't want you to pray for her."

I realized that the woman (I was praying for) was seeing demons. I prayed for her until she was free. She began saying, "Thank you, Lord. Thank you, Lord."

God had brought her back to life and got rid of the demons! Her daughter and others lifted her mother up. God had delivered her completely.

I walked away and was talking to my nephew. A lady came over to me and asked me, "What kind of demons did you cast out of her?"

I said, "She was dead, and God raised her. Just thank God!"

The Lord said to me, "Greater is He that is in you, than he that is in the world."

I was so angry at the woman who had kept rebuking me. If I had listened to her and stopped praying, that lady would have died there.

Months later, I met the lady that had come to me and tugged at me to pray for the lady who had died. She told me what had happened:

She was nearby, and the dead lady's daughter said, "I can't let my mother be dead." She turned to the lady (who had come to me) and said, "Get someone to come and pray."

She had looked up to the platform where the different men were.
She said, "Lord, who shall I get?"

The Lord said, "Get her." (And He led her to me.)

She told me if I hadn't come, she would have dragged me.

Later, on the way back to Orlando, I said to my sister, "Remember last Sunday night when we were at that little country church and a man gave a message over me?" He said God was going to use me in a most unusual way, and when He did, the devil was going to say, "It isn't God."

But it will be God. That is the way it happened. *Praise God*!

Experience 47. House-Sitting Experience
(Chapter 59)

I was living in Florida when I received the letter telling about my family reunion. It was to be held in Michigan in July. I made arrangements at my work to take some time off to attend.

I drove to Michigan and spent a few days with my children and enjoyed visiting with all my relatives.

My brother from Utah came over to me and said he was going to go to Arizona to work for my son Bill who lived there. He wanted to know if I would house-sit for him while he and his wife were gone. He had heard that I had house-sat for others.

I thought he was joking, so I said that I would. This was in July. I left for my return to Florida and forgot all about it.

In September, I got a phone call from him saying they were leaving for Arizona, and they would leave the key for their house with their daughter. I could pick it up from her.

I was shocked! What I had thought was a joke wasn't; he was serious, and he expected me to honor my word. I knew I had to drive to Utah right away. I talked to my boss at work, packed my van, and headed off to Utah. My boss knew that I did a lot of traveling, and he let me work when I was there and always hired me back when I returned.

I arrived in Roy, Utah in September and got settled in.

I quickly found a church. The church was close to the Air Force base, so a lot of the congregation were military personnel. There was hardly an empty seat in any service, as no one wanted to miss anything.

There was such a sweet spirit there. I would help out by playing the piano along with the pastor's wife, who played the organ. I also had lots of opportunities to testify.

I began to attend another church on Sunday evenings and played the organ for their services. The main reason was so I could tell all the wonderful things the Lord had done for me.

The first week in December, I received a phone call from my brother in Orlando, Florida. He called me to tell me that our sister Doetha, who also lived there, had gone to the doctor. The doctor was quite alarmed. After checking her over, he gave her a grim report. Her birthday was in a week, and he didn't think she'd live until then.

My brother Brice said, "You had better pray about coming back here and praying for her; and hurry!"

I began praying immediately after his phone call, and then I felt I should call my friend Erma in Michigan. She was my prayer-partner. I told Erma what Brice had said in his phone call. I asked her to pray too.

Quite often, when we prayed, the Lord would give us a word of instruction in what to do in a given situation. She said she would pray, and we hung up.

In just a short time, the phone rang, and it was Erma. She had heard from the Lord, and He said I should go and pray for Doetha. He would raise her up. She gave me Scriptures for Doetha also.

I called Doetha and gave her the Scriptures and told her I was coming to pray for her. I would be there in a few days.

She seemed quite relieved.

After talking to her, I said to the Lord, "Lord, how am I going to drive there when I only have $40.00? That won't buy me enough gas to get from Utah to Florida. What do you want me to do?" (I hadn't worked for some time, so my finances were low.)

While I was waiting for an answer from the Lord, I thought I'd better call my son Bill and have him tell my brother Arwin that I had to leave his house, and what should I do about it?

He said he would tell him.

A little while later, my brother called and said, "Just leave everything and go. Doetha is more important than the house. Leave the key with my daughter."

Then, Bill called and wanted to know how soon I was leaving.

I told him I was waiting for the Lord to tell me when to leave. (I didn't tell him that I didn't have the money to go. I'd have to wait and see how the Lord would work it out.)

While we were talking, Bill's wife kept saying to him, "Bill, let me talk to your mother."

He kept saying, "No, I'm talking to her."

Well, she finally said, "Ask her if she needs any money."

So he asked me, and I told him that the Lord would take care of it.

He just kept asking me.

I didn't say anything.

Finally, he said, "How about $50.00?"

I didn't answer.

So he said, "How about $100.00?"

I didn't answer again.

So he said, "How about $200.00?"

When he said $200.00, I said, "Stop, stop."

He said, "Okay, Mom, I'll send you $200.00."

I couldn't talk, as by this time, I was crying at how the Lord was working. How long would it take for the money to get here?

It wasn't very long and the phone rang again. Arwin said, "Don't wait for the money. Call Kim and have her go to the ATM and get $200.00 from my account. Bill will give me the $200.00 here."

I called Kim, and she went right to the bank and was back in a few minutes with the money. She and her sister helped me load my van, and within an hour, I was heading down the road to Florida.

Experience 48. Florida, Here I come Again

(Chapter 60)

I drove to the nearest gas station and filled my gas tank and checked the oil-and-tires on my van.

Then I headed to the expressway and began my trip to Florida. This was my second time the Lord had sent me from Utah to Florida. I loved Utah, but it seemed that the Lord only let me stay there for a few months, and then back to Florida.

It was a cold, blustery Sunday morning, and the temperature was hovering around 20 degrees. The sun was shining, but it was quite windy; and there wasn't any snow on the ground.

I drove along for quite a while, just thinking about all that had happened in just the last few hours. As I talked to the Lord, I told Him that I was amazed at how He had worked it all out. All I had to do was obey, and He did the rest. God always has a plan.

A few hours later, I decided that I would stop at the next exit with a restaurant and have lunch. I wouldn't need to stop again until I needed gas.

At the next exit, I turned off, and I noticed a man standing near the area where you would get back onto the expressway. He had on a light, cotton jacket and summer-clothes and tennis shoes. He also had a small bag under his arm.

I thought to myself, "He sure isn't dressed for such cold weather." I was sure he was shivering. I told myself that if he was still there when I came out, I would pick him up.

I went on and had my lunch. As I was leaving, I bought two cans of pop and a few candy bars.

When I arrived back at the highway, the man was still standing there. I drove over by where he was and motioned for him to get in.

He just stood there, so I rolled my window down and asked him if he wanted a ride. He acted strange, like he didn't know what he wanted to do.

When I asked him again, he finally opened the door and got in.

I turned up the heat and asked him where he was going.

He said, "Texas."

I told him I was going through there. (I wondered why he was dressed in such thin clothes when it was so bitter cold out.)

I asked him why he was so hesitant about getting in and riding with me.

He told me that he was a semi-truck driver, and he wasn't in the habit of riding with women drivers: He had always done his own driving.

He noticed my sign on the dash that said, "One way: Jesus."

He said, "Are you a Christian?"

I told him that I was and proud of it.

He told me that he used to be married to a lady preacher. She had really done him wrong. From then on, he thought all Christian women were all alike.

I told him not to judge me by his ex-wife. I wasn't like that, and neither were other Christian women.

He told me that he was born in Kentucky, and his mother was raped when she was 14. He was born from that rape. His mother died in childbirth, and he was raised by his grandparents. His grandfather was a fan of John Wayne, so he named him "John Wayne."

When John Wayne grew up, he joined the military where he spent many years. He had a nice home built for his grandparents, but when he got out of the military, both of his grandparents had died, so he started driving truck.

He met this lady preacher and later they married. She had been married before and had grown children.

He was a long-distance truck driver; and one day, as he was driving through Salt Lake City, something burst in his head. He blacked out. He was involved in a terrible accident and was in a coma for a year or more. He was in a hospital in Salt Lake City.

When he finally came out of the coma, he had no clothes or money, but he did have his memory. He remembered that he had a home in Kentucky. The nurses who cared for him (over the long hospital-stay) went together and bought him some clothes and a suitcase, and he left to go to Kentucky.

He managed to get back to Kentucky and finally returned to his home.

Someone was living there. When he went to the door, a man answered: It was his wife's son. He wouldn't let him in. He told him that his mother had divorced him; and she got the house, so he had to leave. He was devastated!

Now I could see why he didn't trust Christians. He showed me a card that he had to carry with him all the time. It said, if he was found unconscious, it should be reported to the hospital in Salt Lake City, and they would take care of him.

He said the hospital was trying to find a surgery or something that would help him. He kept in touch with the hospital.

He knew he was not to drive, but he didn't know what else to do. He went to the nearest truck stop and would offer to drive trucks from coast-to-coast. He had been doing this for some time before I met him.

The day I picked him up was a Sunday. He had not eaten since Thursday morning. He had gotten a ride with a trucker to help drive from the east-coast to the west-coast. They had stopped near Salt Lake City for breakfast. The driver gave John a token to go and take a shower.

When John came out of the shower, the truck and the driver were both gone. John's suitcase was in the truck, so now John had no clothes except the clothes he had on, and those he wore before he took the shower. His winter coat was in the truck too, so now he just had a light, cotton jacket to wear. He was devastated again, and this is when I came on the scene.

I could see that he was hungry, as he kept looking at the candy bars on the dash. I told him to have a pop and some candy bars, and he refused. He said he couldn't eat them because they were mine.

Finally, I said, "Okay, if I eat one and drink a pop, will you?"

He finally said "alright," but he kept saying that he felt that he was taking my food.

I told him that I felt that the Lord had this all planned: He was at that certain spot and I came along to give him a ride. I was going to Florida and he was going to Texas.

We talked for hours, and I shared with him about the goodness of God and different experiences. He began to see how God had been with him all along. I told him that I was going to stop somewhere and get him a meal, but he refused. He said, "No woman is going to buy me food!"

After a long time, he finally agreed to let me buy him a meal, but we had to wait until we got to Las Vegas. He said he used to drive through there on his regular truck-run, and he knew a place there where you could get all you could eat for just a few dollars.

When we got to Las Vegas, he knew right where to go. He told me where to drive to the restaurant. When we got out of the van. I handed him a twenty-dollar bill and asked him if he would buy me a cup of coffee. He perked right up and began to thank the Lord.

We went inside. After he got washed up, he went to the buffet and took a plate and filled it up. I waited in a booth with my coffee, as I wasn't hungry. He came over and sat down. He looked over at me with tears in his eyes and asked, "Would you pray for me?"

I prayed and he gave his life back to the Lord.

Later, we stopped at the Hoover Dam and stood there looking down at the dam, talking about God and how wonderful He was.

I drove on to Phoenix, Arizona. John said he wanted to wash his dirty clothes and his tennis shoes he was wearing.

I told him that I was going by to pick up my daughter-in-law. She was going to ride with me on to Orlando, Florida. I would drop him off at a laundromat and be back later to get him.

A couple of hours later, I went back to get John. He said that he told someone in the laundromat that he didn't think that I would come back to get him. He thought I was trying to get rid of him. He was surprised when I showed up.

I drove on for a couple of hours and then we stopped. We all had breakfast. John sat in the back seat and slept for the next few hours. When we got near San Antonio, Texas, John said he was getting off at the next truck-stop. I think John left with a different outlook on life.

That night, my daughter-in-law and I stopped at a motel; and the next night, we arrived in Orlando. I had called my brother who lived there, and we spent the night at his home.

The next morning, I drove my daughter-in-law to the airport. She went back to Phoenix. She had just come along so I wouldn't be alone.

When I left the airport, I drove right to my sister Doetha's home. She was waiting for me. We embraced, and she whispered in my ear, "Come into the kitchen and pray for me."

She sat down in a chair and I laid my hands on her and prayed for her healing. She stood up all smiles and said, "Now I am ready to go to lunch. *Praise the Lord*!"

She got dressed, and her husband just kept watching her. She was so bubbly and laughing. We went off to lunch and she was healed.

Jesus had kept His word about healing her. She had a great birthday celebration.

Experience 49. Another Prayer is Answered
(Chapter 61)

It was common knowledge, where I was working, that the boss was having an affair with one of the female employees. This was a "No-No" in the rules from the head office, but I guess the boss didn't think they would ever find out about it.

Our boss was married and had a family. His wife would come into the restaurant from time-to-time. Many times, my boss would ask me questions about Christians and things they did or said. Occasionally, he would ask about a Scripture and what it meant.

I'd tell him the answers and maybe tell him about an experience I had similar to what he had asked about.

One day, he told me that his wife had gotten saved and filled with the Holy Ghost. He said she had really acted different. He wanted to know what had happened to her.

I explained what the Bible said about being born again and the baptism of the Holy Ghost. I could tell that he was trying to understand, but he looked perplexed.

One afternoon, I was working back in the kitchen when one of the employees came to me and said the boss's wife was out in the dining room and wanted to see me.

I got permission to go and talk to her. As I approached her table, she greeted me with a bright smile. She asked me to sit down. I was hoping she wasn't going to ask me about her husband's "hanky-panky."

She said, "My husband talks about you a lot and tells me you are a Christian."

I told her I was.

She went on to tell me about her experience when she was born again and also her baptism with the Holy Ghost. She said she was regularly attending a Full Gospel church. She was just bubbling with the joy of the Lord.

She reached over and took my hand and said, "My husband has been working so hard and has to stay and work late, so he doesn't have time to go to church with me and the children. He tells me that you pray for people. I want to know if you'll pray for him to be saved. I want our family to serve the Lord."

I thought about how he had been lying to her to cover up his affair. Yet she was so concerned about his soul.

I looked at her eager face and said, "Are you willing to pray with me that God will save him at 'any cost'?"

She said, "Oh, yes."

I said, "Now wait a minute. Do you know what can happen when you ask God to save him at any cost?

She just shook her head and waited.

I told her about the time I prayed for my son to be saved at any cost, and in three days he was in jail.

I asked her if she would be willing for God to do whatever He had to do to save her husband.

She got a very determined look on her face, and then she said, "All right, at any cost."

I took both of her hands in mine and we prayed together, "Lord, save him at any cost, and thank you, Lord!"

She thanked me for coming to talk with her. She walked away beaming, and I went back to work.

My boss wasn't even aware that she had been there.

A few weeks went by, and my boss was still having the affair with my co-worker. As I walked into the dining room one morning before opening, I saw several small groups of the employees talking among themselves. When one of the girls saw me approaching them, she came over and asked me if I had heard what had happened.

I told her I didn't know what she was referring to.

She told me the boss had been fired the night before. Somehow the front office must have heard about his affair.

I thought, "Lord, was this part of your plan for him?"

Several weeks went by, and then one morning, as I came into work, the assistant manager came to me. He also was a Christian. He told me he got a phone call from our ex-boss, and he gave him a message for me.

He told him to tell me that the night he was fired, he left feeling real bad, wondering what he was going to tell his wife. As he was driving home, he had to pass the church where his wife attended. He saw that the lights were all on in the church and the parking lot was full of cars. Then he remembered that his wife would be there that night. As he drove by the church, he got the feeling that he should go to the church immediately. He just brushed it aside and kept driving. The feeling wouldn't leave him. At the next exit, he pulled his car off and took a side street and headed back to the church.

When he walked into the church, the preacher was preaching. As the church was full, he found an empty seat in the back. At the closing part of the service, the pastor asked if there was anyone there that wanted to be saved and start a brand-new life living for the Lord. My boss stood up and made his way down to the altar.

You can imagine just how surprised his wife was to see him heading to the altar. Needless to say, he became a new creature in Christ that night and began a new life with the Lord, his wife, and family.

As the assistant manager finished the story, I began to praise the Lord. Then I told him how his wife and I had prayed that he would be saved at any cost.

God knows just what it will take to bring someone to the Savior.

Later, I heard that the company hired him back and relocated him in another part of the state.

The girl (he had been having the affair with) still worked with us. One day, she stopped me as I walked past her in the back area of where we worked. She told me she was so sorry he had been fired because of their affair. She asked me if I had heard that he had become a Christian.

"Yes, I heard what had happened," I said.

She began to cry and said, "You know, I wish I could become a Christian too. I go to church with my daughter, but I know I'm too bad to be a Christian. God doesn't want me."

I took her hand and squeezed it and smiled at her as the tears ran down her face. She was filled with utter despair.

"God does want you; no one is too bad," I explained to her.

People walked by us and probably wondered what we were talking about to make her cry.

What a privilege it was to talk and pray with her and lead her to the Lord. She was instantly transformed. Her face lit up and now the tears were tears of joy. She threw her arms around me and we praised the Lord together.

From that day on, everyone could see the change in her and would ask her about it. She would tell them what God had done for her and her new life.

Experience 50. California

(Chapter 62)

The evening sky was dark, and rain-clouds hung above the California skyline. With the windshield wipers sloshing away, I began watching for an exit to get off the freeway. My cousin (whom I hadn't seen for a few years) lived in Long Beach, and I wanted to spend a few days with her. Not knowing what area she lived in, I slowed down and took the first exit ramp. It was very hard to see with the rain and darkness, so I decided to stop at a gas station.

I hopped out of my van and ran inside to ask if they had a public phone. There were two young men standing there. When I asked about a phone, they just pointed across the street and said there were two phone booths over there.

After thanking them, I hurried out into the rain again. I tried the first phone, but it wasn't working. As I headed toward the second one, I noticed a young black man coming from the same direction.

I rushed inside the booth, dialed the number, and was quickly connected with my cousin. She asked me where I was, so she could give me directions.

I pulled the door open and strained to see the street sign in the darkness, noticing the young man standing just outside the door. I closed the door and told her I was on the corner of "Atlantic," just off the freeway.

She said, "Now I know where you are," and gave me the directions.

As I stepped out of the phone booth, the man said, "Did you think you were on Atlantic? You are on 'Alameda'."

I looked over to the sign and realized it did say Alameda. I said, "Oh dear, how am I going to find Atlantic?"

He said he was going that way and would show me as soon as he made his phone call.

I quickly ran over to my van and climbed inside. As I was drying off, the passenger door opened, and he got in and sat down.

"Oh! I forgot to tell you that I am not driving," he said.

Panic began to grip me. I was a widow in my 40's, with six grown children who had no idea where I was except I was heading for California.

I silently shouted, "Oh God, I have gotten myself into another mess. How are You going to get me out of it?"

With a side glance, I could see this man was well-dressed with a wide-brim hat. Young folks would call him "a real sharp dude!"

193

He pointed in the direction I should drive. I could feel him looking me over. Then, glancing into the back, he saw my bed.

When his attention returned to me, he said, "My, you look nice. Would you like to stop and get some coffee?"

I told him, "No thanks." (I felt like Little Red Riding Hood with the Big Bad Wolf getting ready to eat me.)

Repeatedly, he asked me to stop for coffee and told me how nice I looked.

When I declined, he looked back to my bed and asked me if I was afraid.

I calmly told him I wasn't afraid.

He asked me what I was doing in California, as he must have seen my Michigan license plate.

I told him I was writing a book and possibly would work on it here.

He asked me if I was afraid to be traveling alone.

I assured him I wasn't alone.

When I told him that there were four of us traveling together, he scrutinized the back of the van more thoroughly. A bewildered look crossed his face as he said, "I don't see anyone else."

"I have the Father, Son, and the Holy Ghost with me, and woe unto anyone who tries to harm a hair on my head. God's angels are surrounding me and will take care of me," I assured him.

He thought for a few seconds and then asked, "What are you going to write about in your book?"

"Oh, just things that have happened to me since I have become a Christian," I answered.
"You mean like testimonies?" he questioned.

I knew by that response that he had been in church or around Christians. I kept wondering how God was going to get me out of this situation.

Then, he asked if I was going to write about him in the book.
I said, "Maybe."

With that, he said, "Pull over here, this is where I get out."

I drove over to the curb, and he threw open the door and hopped out. He stood looking at me and said, "Lock your doors; you are in a bad part of town. Just keep going in that direction, and you will be all right!" He shut the door and hurried away.

Reaching over to lock the door, I found he had already locked it.

As I drove away, I was amazed how God had worked it all out. I'm sure that man had something else in mind when he got into the van, but God changed his plans. God tells us to call on Him in time of trouble, and He will help us. This is one of the many times I called.

I drove on and found my cousin Helen's home. We had a wonderful time visiting and sharing memories.

I spent a few days with her and then felt it was time to leave.

Experience 51. The Devil Goes to Sunday School Too.

(Chapter 63)

When I was leaving California, the Lord said, "You have your mother's desk in the back of the van. If you don't go to Utah to see your brother, he will be really unhappy with you, seeing as how you are this close."

So I drove to Utah. (When my mother died, my brother had asked for her desk.)

After I had been staying at my brother's for a week. I had the feeling I was to stay in that area longer. Before I went down to breakfast one morning, I told the Lord that if He wanted me to stay, please have someone say, "I think the Lord wants you to stay longer."

As we were having breakfast, I said, "I think I ought to head back to Florida." I got out a road atlas and asked my brother to mark off a good road-course for me to follow in the wintertime.

He got out a yellow pencil and began marking off a good road-course for me to take.

His wife Virginia was watching us and listening, and she said, "I don't think the Lord wants you to leave yet. Let's get the newspaper and go look for an apartment for you."

I said, "*Praise the Lord.* You said the right thing."

She checked off some within a 10-mile radius. The first apartment she called was about six miles away.

I went to check it out, and she waited for me in the car. As I went in, I told her I would know as soon as I went into the apartment if I was to take it or not: The lord would tell me.

When I entered the furnished apartment, the Lord said, "This is it."

I gave the man the rent money and got a receipt. I went back out to the car, and Virginia immediately said, "The Lord told you to live here, right?"

I told her, "Yes."

After a few months, on the first of April, the Lord told me to pack my things into my van: I was to leave to go back to Orlando, Florida. He didn't say why; I just did what He told me to do.

I got in touch with my sister Doetha in Orlando. She said, "That is great!" The people in our rental apartment are moving out, and you can have it the first of May."

This was one of the five times the Lord had sent me to Orlando.

I went down to Pompano Beach, Florida and spent a few weeks with my daughter Melanie and her family. They were there for the winter

While I was at Melanie's, Doetha wrote and said that our brother Brice had been out spraying his orange tree in the back yard. He felt that some of the spray had landed on his skin, for his face, head, and neck were swollen.

After visiting with Melanie and her family, I drove to Orlando. When I arrived, sure enough, when I saw Brice at the end of April, his head was swollen like a basketball, and his ears looked like little decorations. His eyes were so swollen that they were just tiny slits in his face. He didn't feel any pain except that his skin was too tight.

He was the Sunday school teacher at the local United Methodist Church, and he asked me to play the piano for him. The entire Sunday school service for his age-group was in one room. His students were high school kids, college kids, and Navy personnel, as the Navy base was only one mile away.

That Sunday, Brice told the class about a radio-preacher he heard telling the story of a lady who had a cancer on her face, and how she'd gone up to be pray for.

It so happened that the next Sunday, it was obvious that the lady's cancer was still there. She testified that she had been healed and continued to testify to her healing every week, even though the cancer was growing larger every week.

Some of the men in the church went to the pastor and said, "You had better tell that lady to stop testifying that she is healed. It is embarrassing to everyone. We can all see that the cancer is growing larger every day."

The pastor told them he would see about it.

Well, the next time the lady stood up and testified that she was healed, she said, "It was a year ago when I was prayed for and I accepted my healing. And this morning, when I woke up, the cancer was lying on my pillow."

Her face was spotless. *Praise the Lord*!

After Brice told this story, he asked the class, "If you had something like a cancer on your face that you would see every time you looked in the mirror, do you think you could trust God for your healing and not doubt it?"

Everyone was thinking it over and weighing it. When no one responded, Brice said, "Well, I believe I could!"

Now there he was, with his head swollen beyond normal size. He had been having trouble trying to sleep lying down, so he would sit up in a big chair to sleep.

That Sunday night, Brice was having difficulty breathing during the night. So the next morning, his wife took him back to the skin-doctor he had seen before.

The doctor was shocked at his appearance and sent him right to the hospital. They began to run tests immediately.

That Monday evening, the pastor of our church stopped to see Doetha and me. He said, "I saw Brice today at the hospital."

I asked, "Oh, was he there to pray for someone?"

The pastor said, "No, he was a patient!"

We couldn't believe our ears.

He told us it had to do with all of the swelling.

I was starting a new job the next morning, and since Doetha and I needed to be at work, my brother-in-law Carl bought a tray of fruit and went up to see Brice on Tuesday morning. He was there when the doctor came in and told my brother he had a large cancerous tumor in his upper chest, and it was inoperable. So he had better get his business in order, since he only had a short time to live.

After the doctor left, my brother-in-law was so shocked that he stood up and said, "I'd better leave."

Brice said, "You had better take this fruit with you, as I won't need it."

Carl picked up the fruit and left the hospital.

When I got out of work, my brother-in-law told me what had happened.

I said, "Oh no, Brice is not going to die. Now I know why God sent me back here from Utah."

As it was late when I got out of work, I called the hospital to get permission to go in and see Brice early the next morning. My sister came with me.

When we walked into the room where he was, I said to him, "Okay, Brice, you asked for this!"

He looked at me so shocked and said, "Oh-no I didn't!"

I said to him, "Remember Sunday morning in your Sunday school class when you told the story about the lady with cancer and how God healed her? Then you made the statement that you believed you could trust God to heal you in a similar circumstance?

Well, don't you know the devil came to Sunday school that morning saying, 'Well, Brice, we'll just see about that.'? He gave you the shaft! Now, just because he dumped this into your lap, it doesn't mean you have to accept it. You just throw it back at the devil and tell him, 'No way! I won't accept this!'"

I told him, "Now I know why the Lord sent me back to Florida: just to bug you!"

He looked at me so perplexed.

I told him, "Listen here, Brother, you had better not die, or all the students in your Sunday school class will think you are a liar."

Then, Brice began to tell us about his reaction to the doctor's statement that he was going to die. He thought about not having enough life-insurance for his family and how the thought crossed his mind that, when he was released from the hospital, he would get into his car, drive real fast, and run into a tree and get killed. That way, his family would get twice as much insurance-payment, as it would be an "accident" (double indemnity).

The devil gave him several suggestions of ways to end it all, . . . but then, the Lord dropped a Scripture into his mind. He grabbed his Bible and looked up 1 Corinthians 2:5, . . . "That your faith should not stand in the Wisdom of men, but in the power of God!"

He began to praise the Lord! And I told that-old-devil just where he could go with his cancer and thoughts of suicide! *Praise the Lord*!

Brice had the victory over the whole situation. Now he realized that this was going to be a great healing and also a great testimony for him to share with others and encourage them.

Brice said, "Well, *praise the Lord*! I am not going to die; I'm going to live! *Thank you, Lord*!"

Whenever the doctor came into the room, Brice would say, "Doctor, I am healed. Jesus has healed me."

The doctor would become indignant and say, "Mr. Storey, you are going to die!"

It just so happened that the doctor was a Jew who didn't believe in Jesus and this healing talk.

Brice insisted he be released so he could go and teach his Sunday school class the next Sunday.

With much misgiving, they allowed him to go home for the weekend, but they made him promise that he would come right back in for a biopsy to prove that he had cancer.

Brice told his class, "No matter what the test shows or what I see or what the doctors say, I confess that I am healed!" *Praise God*!

Well, they did the biopsy; and yes, it did prove he had cancer. Brice just kept telling the doctor, "I am healed. *Praise God*!"

The doctors would leave the room in disgust.

Brice was in a room with two other patients, one on each side of him. When my sister and I would go to see Brice, we would get the patients to hold hands and make a prayer-circle with us. We would pray that God would heal these people. They would go home, and a new couple of patients would be in their beds. Of course, Brice would share testimonials, talking about Jesus throughout the day.

The Wednesday after he had been re-admitted, Brice kept insisting that he was healed. (The swelling had gone down.) That evening, an attendant came in with a wheelchair and said, "Mr. Storey, get into this chair. You are going for x-rays."

Brice said, "Why at night? They always take me in the morning. . ." He got into the chair and was wheeled to the x-ray department.

The next morning, the doctor came in with some x-rays, determined that he was going to settle this cancer question once and for all. The doctor said, "Mr. Storey, do you see this x-ray? This is the one we took when you were first admitted. See this tumor?"

He held up the x-ray and outlined the tumor with his finger. Then he held up another x-ray. He said, "This is the x-ray taken last night. See this tumor?" He outlined it with his finger. "You can see that the tumor in last night's x-ray is larger than the first one we took when you were admitted."

Brice said, "I don't care what the x-rays show. Jesus has healed me, and I know I am healed."

The doctor wheeled around and dashed out of the room.

That evening, two men came into his room. One was a friend who belonged to the Full Gospel Businessmen's. The other man had come from a different state to attend the Full Gospel Businessmen's Convention.

The Lord had sent him. He walked over to Brice and said, "You are the 8th one." He told Brice that God had told him to come to this convention, and he was to pray for eight people to be healed. He had only prayed for seven, and he wondered who the 8th one was. Brice's friend asked him to come and see Brice. And Brice was the 8th one. He prayed for Brice and said, "Now, I can go home."

Brice was discharged from the hospital, and the doctor told Brice's wife that he would get thinner and weaker. Soon, she would have to drive him wherever he went.

Brice returned to work immediately. He was a salesman, and since all of his customers had heard he was going to die, they were shocked to see him coming in to get their orders. Everywhere he went, they would ask him what had happened.

He would tell them and take their orders. Then he would travel to the next stop. He was a traveling testimony.

The doctor ordered some treatments for Brice to take. He would go to keep the doctor happy.

After several treatments, Brice was sitting in the waiting room and said to the Lord, "Lord, you know I am healed, and I know I am healed. I am getting out of here. This is just wasting my time."

The Lord said, "Now you just wait a minute. Sit down there! Don't you know that I'm using you as a witness to the folks who come in here every day and also to the receptionist and the folks who give you the treatments? You will continue with the treatments until I tell you it is time to quit!"

Not long after that, Brice talked with his doctor. Brice asked, "Well, Doc, how am I doing?"

The doctor just held up his hand and made a circle with his thumb and forefinger.

Brice said, "Does that mean that the tumor is the size of a fifty-cent piece?"

The doctor replied, "No, it means zero!" He turned and walked away quickly.

It has been years since his wonderful healing, and Brice certainly never got any weaker or thinner!

Experience 52. Back to Michigan
(Chapter 64)

I was back living in Michigan. I was house-sitting and taking care of the dog, as my daughter and her family were on vacation in Hawaii. I was bending over the sink washing my hair when the phone rang.

I quickly grabbed a towel and wrapped it around my head. As I answered the phone, I was surprised to find my son Bill (from Arizona) calling me. He sounded upset. When I asked him what was wrong, he said, "Mom, you need to get out here right away: Steve's dying, and you need to come and pray for him."

Steve (19 years old) was Bill's nephew. Michael, my oldest son, was Steve's father.

Bill went on to tell me Steve had cancer of the liver and was pretty sick in the hospital.

He said that a few weeks earlier, a preacher (that was on TV) was coming to Phoenix to hold a meeting, and he prayed for the sick. Bill had suggested to Steve that he would take him there (to be prayed for) if he wanted to go.

Steve agreed to go.

The night of the service, Bill went to pick Steve up. His mom said he was too sick to go, but when Bill went into Steven's bedroom, Steve managed to get out of his bed. He wanted to go to that meeting and be healed.

When they arrived at the meeting, nearly every seat was taken, but they managed to get two seats.

During the evening, the preacher called up to the front anyone that needed healing.

Steve managed to drag himself up there and waited.

After quite a while and a few people had been prayed for, the preacher said, "Now folks, we are going to change the order of the service, and I'm just going to pray for preachers, so the rest of you can sit down."

So, sick, weak, and discouraged, Steve managed to get back to his seat. He came to the conclusion that God didn't want to heal him.

"Will you come, Mom?" Bill asked again.

I told him I'd get right on the phone and get a flight out as soon as I could. I would call him back with the information.

I called the different travel agencies, and they all closed at noon on Saturday. Finally, I got one where the girl hadn't left yet, and she said she would get me a flight and call me back.

I called my other daughter and asked her if she would help me get ready to go.

She said she would be right over.

I asked her to bring one of her son's gym bags, as I didn't have time to drive home 19 miles to get a suitcase.

She said she would bring it.

The girl called back with the information about the flight to Phoenix from Detroit.

Then, I called the airport shuttle, and they would pick me up in an hour. It was about 70 miles to the airport.

By this time, my daughter Melanie had arrived, and she helped me to pack a bag as I dried my hair.

I called my boss at the hospital to tell her I would be away for a few days.

Melanie said she would take care of Terry's home and her dog for the few days I'd be gone.

Melanie asked me if Steve was going to live, and I told her, "Yes, the Lord says he is going to live."

Within one hour, I was on my way to the airport. That was the fastest I ever had to make arrangements to go anywhere.

I got to the airport and right onto the plane. It was as if it was waiting for me. And we were in the air.

I was seated next to a young lady. She turned to me and asked me where I was going.

I told her I was going to Phoenix to pray for my grandson who was dying.

The lady then began to tell me her problems and asked me if I would pray for her.

I took her hand and prayed about her problems to the Lord.

She thanked me and asked me if I was a missionary.

I told her "No"; I was just a Jesus people.

Just then, the announcement came on: The plane was landing in a few minutes in Indianapolis.

She said, "This is where I get off."

I didn't know we were stopping, and she moved past me and said, "Thanks for praying for me. God must have sent you." Then she was gone.

The Bible says to be instant in-season and out-of-season, so we have to be ready to help whenever we can.

When I got off the plane, my oldest son Michael was waiting for me. Mike had three sons, and Steven was his middle son. Mike was so upset thinking he was losing his son; he could hardly talk.

I told him that Steven wasn't going to die, but he couldn't believe me. He was looking at the circumstances, but I had the word from the Lord.

Mike took me right to the hospital and to Steve's room. I was really shocked when I entered his room. Steve was emaciated and sitting all hunched over a pillow on the lunch-table, gasping loudly for every breath. He had the usual tubes hooked to his arm and his nose, and a tube going from the side of him to a container under the bed.

I said, "I hear that you went to a meeting, and the preacher didn't have time to pray for you. Well, I've come to finish the job."

As I prayed for him, I could just feel that God was doing something great.

Michael was sitting in a lounge chair by Steven's bed, crying as he was so sure that Steve was going to die.

God told me to tell Steve to get his life in order.

Friends and family began to come into his room to have their last chance to see him alive and to tell him good-bye.

Mike and I left, and we went to Mike's home. I kept telling Mike that Steve was going to be all right, but he was still looking at the circumstances, and it did look hopeless. Mike had never seen a miracle before, so I could understand why he felt the way he did.

The next day, Mike and his wife both had to work a half-day, as it was Presidents' Day. So, Bill drove 70 miles to take me to the hospital that morning.

When we walked into Steve's room, we saw a miracle. Steve said, "Hi Uncle Bill; Hi Grandma." He wasn't gasping for breath any longer, and he looked healthy and excited. Laughing, he told us he had eaten his breakfast, and he was feeling real good. He talked to Bill for a long time. He still had all the tubes connected to him, but he was raising his arms as he talked and waving his hands, but he didn't seem to notice.

As it got closer to noon, Bill said, "Steve, we've got to leave, as Cathy has invited us for lunch so she can show Grandma her new house." (Cathy was Bill's daughter.)

I told Bill we should pray for Steve one more time.

Bill said, "I can't pray out loud."

I said, "Well, I'll pray out loud and you can pray silently." So, we laid hands on Steve and prayed; and then told him good-bye and walked out into the hall.

We met Mike coming in the door as we were leaving the hospital. I said, "Mike, you are not going to believe Steve when you see him. He is doing great."

He just said he hoped so and went down the hall to Steve's room.

Bill said, "You know, that really felt good to pray for Steve. I'd like to pray for people."

I told him that it's wonderful to pray for people.

Later, as we were having lunch at Cathy's, the phone rang. They said it was for me.

I said, "Why would anyone be calling me here?"

As I answered, someone said, "Hi Grandma." (It was Steve.)

I asked if he was out in the hall, as he didn't have a phone in his room.

He said, "No, I'm home. After you and Uncle Bill left, several doctors came in, checked me all over, and removed all the tubes and things and said that I could go home." He said the doctors were dumbfounded. (His dad took him home.)

That reminded me of the story in the Bible where the people were crying and wailing at a child's death, and Jesus came along and the child was made whole: Another miracle.

Two years later, I received a call again to go and pray for Steve. This time, the Lord said he wasn't going to live. I flew out for a funeral instead.

Standing by his casket, I asked the Lord, "Where is Steven?"

He said, "He's with Me."

Experience 53. Back in Michigan, My Vision

(Chapter 65)

When I left for church on that warm July morning, it felt like any other Sunday morning. I didn't know that the Lord had a big surprise for me.

As I play the piano for the church services and the piano is situated at the front by the platform, I am sitting where I can look out at the sanctuary where the folks are all seated.

As the singing began, I closed my eyes as I often did to just close everyone and everything out so I can just think on the Lord.

There were five of us musicians up around and on the platform.

I happened to open my eyes and look out at those in the sanctuary, and I was shocked: There were only five people sitting in the audience.

I said, "Oh Lord, there are only 10 people here today. I am so sorry." Then I closed my eyes.

The Lord said, "Open your eyes and look again."

When I looked, I was really shocked: The room was full of angels. They were big, tall, handsome, male angels. They were just standing around talking to each other and smiling. Some were slowly moving around.

There was a small group of them standing and visiting in the right-front side of the sanctuary. Others were going up and down the stairs that led up into the sanctuary. Some were standing in-between the rows of seats.

Then I realized that the other folks that were there apparently didn't see them.

I was so wrapped up in what I was experiencing that I didn't lead off in the next song, and the other musicians wondered what was wrong with me. I know I was trembling and distracted with my vision.

Finally, when the singing and the other preliminaries were over, I went over and sat in the pew near the front where I usually sit.

I looked around, and all the angels were still there and enjoying themselves.

When I looked up at the piano, I saw two angels sitting on the piano bench. They stayed there through the whole service.

I just sat and continued to tremble.

At the end of the service, they were still there, and I said, "Lord, if you want me to say anything about the angels being there, have the pastor say something about angels."

As I listened for the "Word," the pastor said something about angels, and I jumped up and said, "Paul, you just said the magic word."

Then I began to tell them about how we were visited by angels all through the whole church service.

I don't know why they didn't see them. I was the only one blessed by it.

As I left and was shaking hands with people, I was still trembling. Different people mentioned that I was trembling.

I continued to tremble all the rest of the day. I was amazed at the Lord allowing me to see the angels while no one else had.

Experience 54. On the Road Again
(Chapter 66)

216

While attending a home-prayer meeting in Orlando, Florida, the Lord said to me to go to Canada. Me and my two youngest children had only lived in our home in Orlando two years. I told Melanie and Kevin what the Lord said, so we began to pack.

I called a man (in the church we attended) to sell our home, and it sold very soon.

I rented a big trailer. We loaded it with all of our belongings. I had a trailer-hitch installed at the trailer rental store.

Melanie and Kevin drove ahead of me on the highway in her car. I drove my car with the trailer on behind.

When I got as far as Ohio, people in other cars would pull up beside me and frantically point to the trailer. I was traveling on the expressway. When I came to the next exit, I drove up the exit ramp. I was only half way up the ramp when the trailer broke off the back of my car, and the tongue fell onto the ground. God had spared me from a very bad accident.

When I checked the hitch, the man (that had installed it) had only bolted the hitch to the floor of my trunk, which was just a thin metal flooring.

I blocked the wheels on the trailer so it wouldn't roll back down the exit ramp.

I made a phone-call to my son-in-law, and he came and pulled the trailer to Michigan.

When I turned the trailer back into a local dealer, I showed him the holes in my trunk floor.

He just said, "Oh, that is too bad."

I told him, "I thank God for keeping me from maybe having a terrible accident."

He said nothing.

I stored my furniture and waited for the Lord's direction. We were near the international bridge that goes to Canada: Just one mile across this bridge, and you are in Canada.

A few weeks went by, and I had not heard from the Lord about Canada. I said, "Lord, we need to go to Canada so Kevin can get into school."

The Lord said, "You don't have to go. I was just testing you."

I shouted, "Thank you, Lord! I really didn't want to go."

I thought later that I had pulled that trailer more than 1,000 miles with the trailer hitch only bolted to a thing sheet of metal. It could have broken loose in the mountains or when I was driving through Atlanta, Georgia or some other place.

Oh, the mercy of our heavenly Father. He had spared me and maybe others.

Experience 55. A New Home Again in Michigan

(Chapter 67)

I talked to my daughter Terry. I told her the Lord said I didn't have to go to Canada: I could stay in this area. I said, "I need to buy a house here. I have the money from the house I sold in Florida."

She said, "I know someone who does real estate. Would you like me to talk to her?"

I said, "Yes, I need a place in the country: When we have prayer-meetings, there will be a lot of cars, and I will need space."

When Terry came home for lunch, she had a handful of pictures of houses, and all were in the country except one.

I said, "Why did you bring a picture of a house in town?"

She said, "Oh, that's her parents' home, and she is trying to sell it."

She went back to work, and I prayed over the pictures of homes for sale.

The Lord said, "Go and look at the one in the city."

I said, "Lord, I need a place in the country."

He said, "The city house."

I called Terry and said, "Tell the lady I will look at the house in the city"

Later that day, the lady met Melanie and me at the city house. She showed us the main floor and the upstairs. We walked back into the kitchen, and I was standing in front of the refrigerator when the Lord said, "This is your new home."

I said, "But Lord, it is dirty and it stinks."

He said, "This is your new home, and it will be a house of prayer."

I looked over at Melanie and said, "What do you think?"

Melanie just said, "Whatever you say, Mom!"

I told the lady, "I'll take it!"

She was shocked! She said, "Just like that? You will take it? It has been for sale for a long time."

I said, "The Lord said this is our new home, and it will be a house of prayer."

She said, "What are you: a missionary or something?"

I told her I just do what the Lord tells me to do.

Within a week, the people were moved out, and then our work began.

If I had looked into the basement or garage, I would have told the Lord, "No." In the basement, they left bushels of peanuts filled with worms, and the garage was full of newspapers and junk.

Kevin and I were busy hauling stuff out to the curb for the trash man. (Melanie was at work.) We pulled up the carpet, and there were animal-puddle stains on the hardwood floors.

We got everything out of the house. Then I had a folding chair, paint pan, roller and paint brush, and paint.

I was painting the living room ceiling when there was a knock at the back door, and it was around 8:00 p.m. I went to answer the door, and there stood two of my lady-friends, and one was crying. The other lady said, "Can you pray for Sister B.? She has a problem."

I said, "Lord, I am not ready!" Then I invited them in. I removed the paint pan off the folding chair, and Sister B. sat down. I prayed for her and they left.

Whether I was ready or not, the house really became a house of prayer. People called for prayer over the phone. There were letters requesting prayer, and people came to the front and back doors day-and-night. I started a Thursday night "Prayer-and-Praise Time." Folks wanted a place to meet. The street was full of cars, and I had people sitting everywhere. They were in the kitchen, bedroom, on the floor, and even on the stair steps; and when the seats were all full, they were standing. We sang, gave testimonies, praised the Lord, and prayed for others. This happened even before I finished re-doing the house: It really did become a house of prayer.

The little boy from next door came over one day, and he said his grandma wanted to know what kind of parties I had on Thursday nights.

I told him, "We have prayer-meetings, and your grandma is welcome to come."

I never heard from them again.

This went on for seven years.

Experience 56. Called to Fast

(Chapter 68)

For some time, I felt the need to fast and had been delaying getting started. I finally said that this was the day that I would start.

I began spending a lot more time in prayer and waiting on the Lord. I felt that there was something that He wanted to make me aware of, and I needed to be sensitive to His Holy Spirit.

On the sixth night of my fast, I felt the Holy Spirit especially close, and as I lay there in bed, the Lord began to speak to me. I was so thrilled that the Holy Spirit would reveal so many things to me.

This went on for many hours. I thought I should get up and get a pen-and-pad and write these things down, but I didn't want to miss anything He was telling me. I thought I could remember everything when I got up in the morning.

After many hours, I asked the Lord if He could stop telling me all these things: I didn't think I could hold any more. I thought my head was going to burst.

I looked at the bedside clock, and it said 6:30 a.m. The Lord had been talking to me for hours. I realized that I wouldn't be doing any sleeping, so I got up. I went out and sat in my rocking-chair in the living room. I asked the Lord why we weren't seeing miracles like those that had happened in the Bible.

The Holy Spirit began talking to me again. He said that Christians don't use the authority that God has given them. He said Jesus gave the authority to the disciples when He sent them out in the sixth chapter of Mark. He gave us this same authority when He went into Heaven and sent the power of the Holy Ghost.

When we received this power of the Holy Ghost "infilling," we also are given the commandment to "go and preach the Gospel, heal the sick, cast out demons, raise the dead, cleanse the lepers; freely you have received, freely give." (Matthew 10:7-8) He also said that greater things that we will do than He did.

What are we waiting for? He has told us what to do, and we sit around doing nothing except talking about all the things that we hear others are doing. And we do nothing. . . nothing!

The Holy Ghost really began to open my eyes to what we should be doing. I thought to myself, "No wonder things aren't happening: I'm not doing what He said in the Bible to do."

When God saved me and I was born again, I told Him that I would do anything He told me to do, and here I hadn't really been doing all these things. Oh, I had done some of them, but if I and others would really get going all-out for the Lord, we could make a big change in the area where we are living.

Then, the Lord began to show me about cancer. Most people are filled with fear-and-dread when they hear someone has cancer. They usually think that person is going to die. Quite often, they do, but they don't have to.

It seems like, on a lot of news on TV, the report is that they've found something else that has a cancer-producing agent in it: It is in our foods, in the air we breathe, in the products they put in and on the ground, and in our water. There is very seldom a day goes by that we don't hear the word "cancer" spoken in our range of hearing. What are we to do?

The Lord told me to look at my forearm (fore-arm).

I did, and I had a vision:

On my arm, I saw a leach, which is a blood-sucking parasite. It seemed to be chewing and sucking on my arm, and the spot was growing bigger and deeper. Quietly and quickly, this thing was eating up my arm.

The Lord said that it was a cancer-demon, and this is the way they operate in and on a person's body.

I asked the Lord what I should do about it, and He said that I should knock it off with the name of Jesus.

I looked at that thing working so quietly and yet so destructively, and I shouted, "In the name of Jesus, get off my arm!"

The thing disappeared off of my arm.

I thought to myself, "We let these cancer-demons eat away at our friends and loved-ones; and we just stand back and say, "Isn't it awful; so-and-so has cancer."

We just let the devil go ahead and destroy their bodies. God has given us authority to get rid of these things.

As I sat there (in the rocking-chair), the Lord said to me, "You know that the same thing is in those tomatoes down in the basement."

A few months earlier, my daughter Melanie came over with a bushel of tomatoes to can. We canned 21 quarts and put them down in my basement, as she didn't have room at her place.

A few months later, I noticed that the tomatoes were all spoiled. Several of the jars had thick furry chunks of mold on them and was pushing the lids up and off of the jars. I thought, at the time, that it was a shame to lose all of those tomatoes. I really didn't know how to dispose of them, so I just turned around and went back upstairs. I thought, maybe later, I would think of what to do in the situation.

Isn't that just like all of us? When we don't know what to do, we just try to forget it, and I guess we think it will go away.

As the Lord was telling me that the same demon was in those tomatoes, I jumped up and said, "That is right, Lord."

I ran to the basement stairs and rushed down to the area where the shelves were that held all of those rotten tomatoes. I pointed at the jars and shouted with authority, "In the name of Jesus, I command you to be made pure, whole, and good!" I turned around and hurried back up the basement stairs.

Several weeks passed, and every time I would go near the jars of tomatoes, I would look at them; and they didn't look any different to me: They were still poking up out of the jars, and mold was still on them. The last time I was down there, it was the day before New Year's.

I had been invited to a New Year's evening service. I felt that the service was kind of dull, so I asked the Lord to give us a miracle in the service tonight.

There was a good crowd that night, although we were having a snow-storm. When it was my turn to play my accordion and sing, I told them about the Lord talking all the night before and how the Lord showed me about cancer and how I prayed for the tomatoes in my basement. (That wasn't received very good.)

Later, they had a lunch; and then it was midnight, and everyone gathered around the front and began to praise the Lord for another year.

Off to my left, there was a lady, and she began to sway; and then she fell to the floor. The pastor said, "Oh, Sister Miller has just been slain in the Spirit."

I leaned over her and saw that her eyes were rolled back in her head and her mouth was open. I got down beside her, and I could see that she wasn't breathing.

I said, "Lord, she is not breathing."

He said, "I know: You asked for a miracle tonight."

I said, "I know, but it won't be a miracle if she is dead."

He said. "You know what to do!"

So, I put my hands on her and began to pray fervently.

After a bit, she began to move and cried out repeatedly, "I want my Jesus; I want my Jesus."

I told her she would see Jesus again, but He still had more work for her to do.

I don't believe anyone else realized what had happened, but I knew that I got my miracle that night.

One evening, I was sitting in my living room reading, and the Lord spoke to me and said, "When are you going to try those tomatoes?"

I told the Lord that I had already had supper and wasn't hungry.

He just kept asking me, "When are you going to try those tomatoes?"

I jumped up and said, "Okay, Lord, I will do it right now." I went down in the basement and over to the shelf that held the rotten tomatoes. I picked two of the very worst moldy jars of tomatoes and carried them upstairs. I took the jars over to the kitchen sink and spooned off the mold and other parts that looked bad. Then I tasted them: Wow! They tasted like fresh-cooked tomatoes. I got out some hamburger and decided to make some Spanish Rice. I poured the remains of both jars in and let it cook with the rice and hamburger and onions. It smelled so good as it was cooking that I wished I had someone else there to let them see that I was cooking rotten tomatoes.

About that time, the phone rang. I hurried and answered it. It was my friend Clare telling me that he had some new records, and he was going to stop by and let me hear them.

"Hurry on over," I said and headed back to the kitchen.

As I passed the stereo, I remembered that the stereo wasn't working, so I just laid my hands on it and said, "I command you to work right."

As I got in front of my refrigerator, I thought, "You are not working right either." I laid my hands on it and commanded it to run properly too.

I just figured that, if God could heal rotten tomatoes, He could fix a stereo and a refrigerator.

I went back to the pan of Spanish Rice cooking merrily on the stove. The food was done, and I set it off the burner, as there was a knock at the door.

As I opened the door, Clare said that something smelled good.

I told him to come out into the kitchen.

He asked me if I was just now going to eat supper, and I told him that I'd already had supper; but the Lord asked me when I was going to try the rotten tomatoes, and so I cooked a dish with rotten tomatoes. I asked him to sit down and eat with me, and he just looked at me with revulsion and said, "No thanks, I have already had supper."

No amount of persuasion would change his mind. He did consent to sit at the table with me and watched me eat my dish of food.

After I finished eating my prayed-for tomatoes, I put the records on the stereo, and they all payed just fine. The refrigerator was functioning just fine as well.

Clare kept watching me and asked several times if I felt all right.

I told him I was, "Fine," as the Lord had made the rotten tomatoes good.

A while later, when he left, he asked me again how I felt, and I told him, "Fine."

The Lord was showing me that we can do anything in His name, and we have all authority to do anything.

Why are we so afraid to try something for God? We have gotten so soft with the devil that we pet him rather than stamp our foot and commanding him to leave us alone. Jesus told me, one day, that the devil can only roar. If we resist him, he will flee. (James 4:7)

Why do we allow him to intimidate us? We have all the power in the name of Jesus. God is making us aware of our short-comings, and we had better get into the Word and find out who we are and who we have in us. When a cold germ comes by us and begins to attack us, do we say, "Oh Dear, I think I am catching a cold."? Or, do we say, "Hey, you cold germ, get out of here in the name of Jesus!"? Just say, "I plead the blood of Jesus over me, and you can't bother me with any sickness." It works; I have done it.

Let us learn the word of God and then use it in our everyday living. We accept all the things that the devil puts on us and then wonder why this has happened to us.

People, we have no one to blame but ourselves. What you accept from the enemy is your problem. If you had read the Bible, you would see that it says, "The enemy is out to kill, steal, and destroy." (John10:10) Don't think that, if you are nice to him, he will go away and let you alone. That is not how he operates. He is out to destroy you and kill you.

He would like nothing better than to steal your money too. After he has attacked you physically and you have allowed it, you have to use your hard-earned money to try to get some relief. You carry your money to the drug store and buy things to make you feel better or just run to the doctor and pay him a lot to make you feel better. Wouldn't it have been better if you had resisted and took authority in the first place and save you all the misery and loss of money?

I and others ate every single jar of those rotten tomatoes except for one can we couldn't get open. No one got sick! *Praise God*!

Experience 57. A Family Reunion

(Chapter 69)

Driving along the highway that warm July day, heading for my family reunion, I never dreamed that God was going to perform a miracle at that gathering.

I just relished the pleasant beautiful day. There wasn't a lot of traffic, so I could let my mind wander a little as I drove along.

First, I was thinking of my brothers and sisters that I hadn't seen for quite a while. We were from a very large family, so when we got together, there was a lot of catching up to do.

Mom and Dad had 13 children, and there were 10 of us left. Mom had gone to be with the Lord, and Dad had followed her 13 years later

I was the tenth child and had three younger brothers. My brother next younger than me had been killed in the Korean War, and the other two children had died at a very early age.

Mom had prayed for us all to give our lives to the Lord for many years before she died, but we all were not in the fold yet.

It took me over three hours to get to the picnic grounds where the reunion was being held, but I didn't think that was too far to drive, as some of the others had driven or flown-in from other states as far away as 2,000 miles.

When I drove in the drive to the park, I could see lots of children running around. The adults were carrying ice chests and dishes and lots of goodies that we would all be enjoying before too long. There were lots of hugs and handshaking and pats on the back as we all greeted each other. Some of the youngsters were hard to recognize, as they had grown and changed so much.

As we were just standing around talking, I noticed my oldest brother's wife Laura Mae coming toward me. We just talked small talk for a few minutes, and then she began to tell me that she was going to be going to the hospital for surgery.

I knew that she had a lot of health-problems for most of her married life.

When she said that she was to be operated on soon, I just told her that we would have to pray for her before we all left that day. I was surprised when she agreed to being prayed for, because she never seemed interested when any of us talked about the Lord.

We had a great day and ate too much and talked for hours. Then, I noticed that some of the folks were packing up their picnic supplies and leaving to go home.

I asked someone where my sister-in-law had gone.

They said she was sitting out in their camper.

I went over and asked her if she would come and let us pray for her. She came with me and sat down.

We gathered around her. By this time, there were only a few of us there. We were all born-again believers except my brother Harry, her husband. He stood off to the side a little way to observe.

I don't believe they had ever gone to church much. I didn't think she had ever had a group of Christians descend on her and pray with the laying on of hands as we were doing at this time.

We all prayed for her, some praying out loud and others silently.

I don't recall what the others were praying, but I was praying that God would heal her from top to bottom. And I prayed that she would receive a born-again experience and a new heart: *Lord*!

She began to weep and then said, "I'm healed."

I told her, "What you say is what you get; and also, it says in the Bible that we overcome by the blood of the Lamb and the word of our testimony. Thank God for your healing."

In the meantime, my brother Harry was standing nearby, holding a big red handkerchief and crying and blowing his nose.

The others all went outside, so there was just my brother and I left. I walked over to where he was standing, and he began to thank me for healing his wife.

I said, "I didn't heal your wife; God did! I can't heal anyone. We pray and God does all the rest. We are just His glove, and He is the powerful hand in the glove."

He was still crying, and I looked into his face and I said, "Harry, aren't you sick-and-tired of the old life that you're living?"

He said, "Yes, I am sick-and-tired of this old life that I am living."

I said, "Well, just ask God to give you a new life."

I repeated it again for him to tell God to give him a new life.

He just kept saying "Yup" and cry and blow his nose in that big red handkerchief.

Well, we gave each other a big hug, and everyone let that picnic grounds a lot happier that evening.

My brother and his wife had never come to visit me, as they lived quite a distance away, but the next Saturday, I heard a knock on my door; and when I opened it, there they stood. They were smiling from ear to ear.

When my sister-in-law Laura Mae came in, she had her arm extended above her head, and she said as she waved her arm back-and-forth, "Do you know what this is?"

I said, "No, I don't know what this is."

She said, "This is the arthritis I had since I was 29 years old, and it is gone. I am also healed from the thing that I was to have an operation for, and I have no more headaches or anything. I don't need any pills for anything." *Praise the Lord*!

She was so happy that she was just beaming. . . and Harry was a changed man too.

God had given them both a born-again experience, and they were starting a brand-new life. Isn't God Good!

Harry said they would like prayer again, so I pulled out a chair from the dining room table and told them both to each take a turn in the "hot-seat," and God blessed them again.

A few weeks later, there was another knock on my door, and it was them again with another lady. "Would you pray for our friend? She needs help too," they said.

That was the beginning of a happy walk with the Lord for them; and they began to go to church, buying tracts and passing them out, and telling people what God had done for them.

You never know how or when God is going to answer your prayers for salvation or healing (for others), but it's always right on time; and God has everything all set up for us to see and experience a miracle!

Experience 58. Time for a Good Spanking
(Chapter 70)

I was living back in Florida when my son Bill called me from Michigan and told me that my youngest son Kevin had appendicitis and was in the hospital about to be operated on. Bill asked if I could come right away.

I told him I'd call the airlines and get a flight out as soon as possible. I booked a flight that was to leave within a few hours, and I called Bill to tell him when I'd get to the airport.

By the time I arrived at the hospital, the operation was over, and Kevin was back in his room. I spent the next few days visiting him at the hospital. Eventually, I took him back to his apartment and got him settled in.

I then went to Port Huron, Michigan to visit my two daughters.

Early the next morning, one of my friends called to ask if I'd like to drive into Canada for a breakfast-meeting to hear a Christian speaker who had a very interesting testimony about angels.

Suddenly, that still, small voice inside of me said loudly, "Bryson City, North Carolina." I was in shock. Taking out a piece of paper, I wrote the name down.

The man I had come with looked at me. I must have had a startled look on my face, because he whispered, "What's the matter, Donna?"

I just pushed the paper over to him and said, "This is where I have to go next."

He read the name and asked me if I'd ever been there before: Did I know anyone there?

I told him, "No."

I wanted to leave immediately for Florida to get my van and start for North Carolina; but then, I thought these people were good enough to bring me to this meeting, and I shouldn't ask them to take me back to my daughter's place before the meeting was over, so I stayed.

When I got back to my daughter's, she said she was so happy I was there and asked if I could stay a few days.

Feeling guilty that I had just arrived the day before, I thought I'd better stay longer. I left a week later.

When I landed in Orlando and went back to my apartment, I thought about telling my sister and brother-in-law about my leaving. Then I recalled what my brother-in-law once told my sister, "I don't think God talks to Donna and tells her to go to these different places: I think she just likes to run around."

I decided I'd wait a while before saying anything to them since I was renting an apartment from them. So, a couple of weeks went by, and I finally told them that I had to leave.

My sister said her husband was real upset, because he thought I wouldn't come back.

I told her I'd pay a month's rent in advance, and then I left.

I had no problem getting to Bryson City. I drove around the town and finally drove up onto the side of a hill and stopped, parked, and then asked the Lord, "Well, I am here, Lord. What do you want me to see or do? Why am I here?"

He said, "I told you to come three weeks ago."

I began to sputter . . . "Well, Lord, You know I stayed to visit my daughter, and then it took time to tell my sister and her husband about . . ."

He said, "Yes, but I told you to come three weeks ago."

I asked, "You mean, I came here for nothing? This has been a dry run?"

"No, He said, "you are here for a purpose. I am teaching you a lesson!"

When I asked Him what the lesson was, He said, "I want you to do what I say when I say it, not when you feel like it or when it is convenient."

I felt terrible. I knew I should have come sooner.

Since the next day was Sunday, I thought I'd stay overnight and go to church.

The next morning, I walked into the church. It felt rather strange. The folks standing at the front door (greeting people) acted as if they hadn't seen me, so I just went inside the sanctuary and found a place to sit. I tried to enter into the service, but it felt strange to me.

When the service ended, the pastor and his wife were at the door shaking hands as people were leaving. I stood there in front of them waiting for their handshakes, but it was as if they didn't see me. Finally, I just walked out. I decided it was time to head back to Orlando.

Later, I stayed overnight in Florence, North Carolina. In the morning, I turned on the radio in the van and heard the news that a hurricane was coming. I thought I'd better hurry back to Florida.

That evening, it was raining really hard, and the wind was blowing violently. It was very dark, and it became difficult to see.

The trees were bending over nearly touching their tops to the ground, and the rain was coming down in sheets.

All of a sudden, a man and a teenage boy were standing in the middle of the road, waving their arms for me to stop.

I slammed on the brakes, wondering what was wrong. There was a semi-truck standing by the side of the road

They ran around to the passenger side and pulled the door open. The man said, "I ran out of gas. Could you give us a ride to the truck-stop? It is in the direction you are going."

They got in; they were soaked. The man said the places he passed were closed, and he had thought he could find a place, but ran out of gas.

It seemed that various places were closed and boarded up against the hurricane. Finally, we came to a little place with a wrecker and a few gas pumps. They thanked me and got out, saying they could get a ride back.

I drove on a few miles and found a big truck-stop. There was a restaurant, and the parking lot was full of cars and some trucks.

I found a parking place and ran toward the restaurant, hoping to get a cup of coffee. I noticed the windows were boarded up too. I hurried inside. The place was packed, and the driving rain was coming in around the door; and men with buckets were scooping it up and throwing it back outside.

I found a place to sit down and noticed the truckers all had really large flashlights sitting on the tables. Before a waitress could come over to me, all the lights went out. Immediately, the big flashlights came on and lit up the room.

I sat there for a few minutes and then decided I might as well go out and go to bed in my van. The van was rocking from the gusts of wind and rain, but I went to sleep anyhow. During the night, I woke up, and it was still storming and blowing, so I just went back to sleep.

When I awoke in the morning, it was a bright sunny day. The storm was over, and the parking lot was empty except for me.

I looked out my back window and was shocked. One of those big I-beam signs (that advertise gas by the side of the expressway) had bent over, and the top of it was just a few inches from the back of my van.

I thanked God for keeping me safe through the storm. Then I thought of what would have happened if that sign had been a few feet closer. *Thank you, Jesus*!

I headed home, and when I got near Daytona Beach, Florida, I noticed my van was starting to sway. Thinking it was windy, I looked at the palm trees to see if they were swaying, but they were perfectly still.

That's when I realized I had a flat tire. I drove over to the side of the road and stopped. The rest of the traffic was flying by on the expressway.

Sure enough, my right back tire was completely flat.

It was 97 degrees outside, and I noticed I was nearly out of gas, so I thought it best not to run the air conditioner. The love bugs were thick, so I didn't care to roll down the windows.

Where were all the police cars I had seen on the highway? They'd all disappeared, and so I prayed for help, . . . but no answer.

Taking the little car jack out of the van, I tried to put it under the back axle, but it kept tipping over. Since I had on a dress and nylons, I decided that, if I was going to crawl under the van to get the jack set up, I had better go take off my nylons. (The surface where I was parked was covered with hot black tar [i.e., hot from the hot sun]).

In a few minutes, I was back outside crawling under the van and finally got the jack to stand up. (I burned both of my knees, and they began to blister.)

As I took the tire and wheel out of the back door, I was murmuring all the time, "Hey Lord! Where is my Good Samaritan? I helped those guys last night when they ran out of gas."

". . . . (*Silence*)"

It didn't help any that I just had all the tires rotated, and they had put them on with an air impact wrench. Do you think I could get those lug nuts loose? I'd work on them for a while and then I'd climb back inside the van out of the sun, complaining loudly.

Finally, after 2 ½ hours, I got all the lug nuts off and was going to pull off the wheel when up drives my Good Samaritan: a big semi-truck containing beer and a tanker truck. The two drivers ran up to me. One said, "Lady, you shouldn't be doing that!"

By the time they arrived, I was nearly in tears feeling sorry for myself.

Within minutes, they pulled off the wheel and popped the other one on, put it back together, and threw the flat into the back of the van.

I tried to pay them, but all they would accept was my thanks and my joy at having it completed.

When I arrived at home, my brother-in-law asked me why I had to go to North Carolina, and I told him that I went there to get a good spanking. That made him happy.

From then on, I didn't hesitate when the Lord said to go. I just went and asked questions later.

Experience 59. My Vision I had in Florida; My Blue Van

59a. Chapter 71

The Lord gave me a vision of what was coming in this world when I was in Florida:

I saw the sky full of dark clouds. Then I saw a huge black cloud rolling toward me, and the Lord said, "Warn the people about the destruction that is coming!"

Then the scene changed. . ..

I saw two large hands holding the earth. The hands began to slowly sway sideways, like a pendulum on a clock: Very slowly, back and forth.

The hands were holding the earth. The Lord said, "I am going to shake the earth from side to side. Not man, but I am." As He was moving the earth side to side, the earth began to crack, like a jigsaw puzzle. The pieces began to flutter down.

Then the Lord said, "Warn my people that the days are going to be so evil that, if they don't stay close to me, they won't make it through."

59b. Chapter 72

Many of these stories happened when I had my blue van. Most of my long trips have been made in my blue van.

I have moved from Michigan to Florida five times. I have moved to Utah two times, off to California once, and once to Arizona.

The Lord told me to buy that van after He had sent me back to Michigan from Florida. After that, many trips were taken in the van.

Finally, He sent me back to Michigan from Arizona. That was my last trip.

I got a job in a hospital in Michigan. One Sunday morning, as I walked outside to go to work, I walked over to where I had parked my van the night before... *No van!* Just an empty parking spot where I had parked it.

At that time, I was living in an apartment complex, and I had an assigned parking spot. All the other cars were in their assigned spots, but mine was empty.

I thought, "Maybe I'm dreaming!" I went back into my apartment. I looked in the bathroom, and the shower was wet where I had taken my shower. I could see where I had eaten a quick breakfast.

I walked back outside and over to my parking spot. . . *No van!*

I went back inside and called my daughter Melanie. When she answered, I said, "Did I loan you my van and forget about it?"

She said, "What are you trying to say, Mother?"

I said, "My van is gone."

She said, "We'll be right over."

Then I called the Sheriff Dept. They came right over. The officer made out the report.

My daughter Melanie and her husband Philip talked to the officer. There had been a lot of robberies in this area, and they thought someone had taken my van to haul things away in.

We all looked for that blue van, but it was never found.

That was the last of my traveling for the Lord. I had traveled to many places, put on lots of miles, and saw a lot of people. I saw many prayers answered also.

After 20 years of answering the Lord's call, I am back home near my kids. (Two of my children live in Arizona, but I hear from them all the time.)

One day, several months after the van was stolen, my little grandson Tim said, "Well, I guess the Lord wants you to stay here, Gram: Your van is gone!"

My grandchildren still talk about Gram's blue van. They loved to ride around in it.

*** The End ***

April 21, 2018